Baby Boomers

Helen Townsend is a product of the post-war baby boom, vintage 1947. She grew up in suburban Melbourne and Sydney in a typical middle class family with four children, one Scotch terrier and one car. She excelled at hula hooping and nursed a fierce desire to invade her brothers' tree house. At Killara Primary School she learnt running writing, the chain stitch and more than she needed to know about the British Empire. She wore a hat and gloves for five years at Hornsby Girls High School where she completed the leaving in 1964. She then went to Sydney University.

She is now a full-time writer, living in Sydney. She has been happily married for seventeen years to the same man. They have two children aged 16 and 12. They live in a three bedroom suburban home, have two cars, two cats, a killer budgie and a blue tongue lizard.

To my Mum and Dad who provided
the 26 inch Malvern Star, the
hula hoop and lots, lots more.

BABY BOOMERS

First published in Australasia in 1988 by
Simon & Schuster Australia
7 Grosvenor Place, Brookvale NSW 2100

A division of Gulf+Western

National Library of Australia
Cataloguing in Publication data

Townsend, Helen.
  Baby boomers

  Includes index.
  ISBN 0 7318 0032 X.

  1. Baby boom generation — Australia.
  2. Australia — Social conditions — 20th
  century. 3. Australia — Social life and
  customs — 20th century. I. Title.

994.05

Front cover photograph courtesy of Mrs G. M. Semmler
Back cover photograph courtesy of the Bertinshaw family

Designed by Helen Semmler
Typeset in Hong Kong by Setrite
Printed in Australia by Globe Press Pty Ltd

Baby Boomers

Growing up in Australia in the 1940s, 50s and 60s

Helen Townsend

SIMON & SCHUSTER

AUSTRALIA

Foreword

'What's a baby boomer?' asked my 13-year-old son.

'Someone who grew up after World War II when there were lots of babies born. By the way, did you know that our milkman used to deliver the milk in a horse and cart? I used to help him when I was your age. The horse's name was Nugget. It was more convenient than driving a van. The horse knew the milk run better than the milkman.'

'Dad, I'm just going out to do some skateboarding.'

'Just a minute son. The milk was dippered out of big churns into saucepans and billies people left outside their front doors. My mother used to scald the milk on the stove, and scrape off the clotted cream that rose to the top.'

'I told Matthew I'd meet him up the lane five minutes ago Dad.'

'Sure son. One day my mother noticed some funny dark stuff in the bottom of the milk jug. It always seemed to be there. She kept asking my father to take it to the Health Department for analysis, but he just kept saying it was probably all right. When the milk was investigated, the dark stuff was identified as dead pus cells. The milkman's cows had mastitis...'

I was speaking to the echo of a slammed door.

But I defy any baby boomer to dip into Helen Townsend's book and not start burning with nostalgia. The bulk of the material was gleaned from a series of dinner parties, where guests were encouraged to discuss their school days, ('You'd have your vegemite sandwich in a brown paper bag. On hot days it'd curl round the edges'),toys, games, sex, ('I found a condom on the beach and innocently put it in my shell collection. My parents were too embarrassed to enlighten me') and other rites of passage. They must have been hilarious affairs. The reminiscences also detail an Australia that is as foreign to today's young people as stories of the horse and buggy era were to us baby boomers.

'One of the boys in our school was American and he actually admitted he liked folk dancing. It finished him. It was as bad as admitting you liked girls.'

'Running through the girls' toilets was the most incredible dare. And thrilling – all those little girls screaming!'

'We had a hymn about "Gladly the cross I'd bear for Jesus." I sang it for years, wondering about the connection between Jesus and the cross-eyed bear.'

Enough! This is a foreword, not a review. Still, I'd have given a lifetime's collection of chipped tombolas to have been at some of Helen Townsend's research dinner parties. It is faintly disquieting to realise one's own childhood and early life is now an era of interest to oral historians. However the post-war years – particularly memories of childhood – are not well documented. Perhaps this excellent compendium of experiences will trigger others to explore memories of a vanishing Australia.

The book brought me great joy, but marital discord. I began reading it in bed at night, cackling out loud, and quoting extracts to my partner of twenty years. My sincere advice to fellow baby boomers and other readers is not to do this.

Anyway, as Fred Dagg often says, 'I'll get out of your way.'

Tim Bowden

Contents

The Baby Boomers

Remember M
Remember E
Put them together
And remember ME.

The baby boomer's childhood was the childhood of billycarts, Vicks VapoRub, box-pleated tunics and Smokey Dawson. It was the childhood of cubbies, the Argonauts, musk sticks and 'God Save the Queen'. It was the childhood of the two-parent family and the three bedroom suburban home. It was the childhood with Mum cooking Anzac biscuits for afternoon tea. It no longer exists.

A whole generation of Australians shared that childhood. Baby boomers are people who grew up in the second half of the 1940s, and the 1950s and 1960s. Officially, the term, 'post-war baby boom' refers to the increase in births when Australian servicemen returned home from World War II. It was a time when couples who had deferred marriage got married. They were keen to establish families. Couples separated by war were anxious to complete their families. Post-war reconstruction not only involved large national projects, but dealt vigorously with bread-and-butter issues such as housing for families, child endowment and better maternity hospitals. Australians, having the good fortune to be on the winning side of the war, wanted to settle down to normal, ordinary, everyday living. This normal, ordinary everyday environment shaped the childhood of children born in the 1940s, 1950s and early 1960s.

The normality and common placeness lasted until the late 1960s. It was an era of great political stability and increasing prosperity for Australians. Sir Robert Menzies was Prime Minister from 1949 until 1966. His fervently pro-British nationalism and sleepy social and political

Mum, Dad and the kids outside their three bedroom brick home.

Afternoon tea was a ritual for children as well as adults.

conservatism was indelibly stamped on the nation.

The previous generation of Australians had grown up in a period of acute economic depression and had then had to face the uncertainty of war. The baby boomers grew up in a period of certainty and security. Although Australians were aware of the Korean War, the Suez crisis, the Cold War, the Berlin Wall and the threat of nuclear war, they were strangely insulated. By today's standards, they were fairly sexist, racist and very British. Their major pre-occupations were home and family and material comfort. The nation was increasingly middle class, interested in owning homes and cars. Red brick suburbia spread relentlessly.

As a nation, Australians had no great dreams or visions. They imported migrants so they could work in the factories and learn to be Australian. They built the Snowy Mountains Scheme so there would be enough electricity for every woman's steam iron and new stove. Children were educated so they would have good, safe jobs. How many links in a chain, how many chains in a mile, how many pence in a pound? Recite 'The Man from Snowy River'.

Australians cultivated the trappings of respectability. The baby boomers had a clean, neat, well-dressed childhood. Most Australians liked royalty and went to church because it was the right thing to do. There may have been a few private misgivings, and there were, thankfully, the larrikins and doubters. The children, of course, didn't always take the adults seriously. But there was a safe, solid set of beliefs always in the background.

More than anyone else, Mum, who worked at home, created the environment for the baby boomer childhood. Mums provided basic food and shelter. If your Mum wasn't home, the one next door would do. The baby boomer was given the freedom of the suburb because there were mothers on every street, in every house. They created a network where everyone knew everyone else. They were the reason you didn't have to lock up.

Behind every mother was a father. There were, of course, the war widows, and everyone felt sorry for them. There were fathers who disappeared mysteriously, never to return. But in general, mothers and fathers came appropriately paired. They didn't have much choice. Social security didn't look after single-parent families. Married women were barred from many jobs and were paid less than anyone else if they were allowed to have them. Adultery and cruelty were the grounds for divorce. Divorces were reported in lurid detail in the evening newspapers. Most couples chose to stay together.

The double-headed figure of the parents reinforced the demarcation between children and adults. In the eyes of children, parents fell in with the rest of the adult world — headmasters, teachers, ministers, scout masters and shopkeepers. It was us and them, often, us versus them. In dress, in behaviour, in recreation, children lived in a world of their own and ten-year-olds did not wear designer labels. Children did not choose their own hairstyles. Short trousers to long trousers, plaits to perms, you were either grown up or you weren't.

Nobody pondered the process of growing up, thought about what went on in a child's mind or attempted to understand it. The most important thing from an adult point of view was that the child grew straight, did his or her homework, and behaved reasonably. The most important thing in a child's mind was that he or she didn't

For the baby boomer, it seemed the safety and security of childhood would last forever.

get into trouble, and could go out and play without spending too much time on homework. The real business of childhood was with other children — in school, on the streets, listening to the radio, watching TV and going to the movies. It was the foods we all hated and loved, the toys we coveted, the books we read, the organisations we belonged to, that bonded us together. It was the painful experiences of sex and growing up, the myths and legends we shared. These are the things that are described in this book.

For every human being, childhood is a magical, if sometimes painful time. It is a time when we absorb experiences, before we try and structure them. It is the time in our lives when we are the least self-conscious and the most our real selves. There is a special pleasure in looking back.

Each generation has its own particular childhood. The childhood of the baby boomers was very different from that of children who grew up in the Depression, or from the Edwardian or Victorian childhood.

Every era of childhood has to end. Not only do the children grow up, but they decide they want to be different. When the baby boomers grew up, some of them preached peace and love and opposed conscription for Vietnam. Others fought in Vietnam. The baby boomers renounced short back and sides, grew their hair and wore strange clothes. They travelled to places like India and Tibet, used decimal currency instead of pounds, shillings and pence. They watched men walk on the moon instead of marvelling at monkeys in satellites.

Some of the baby boomers eschewed mortgaged life in the suburbs and became the truth and beauty seekers of the 1970s. They questioned the house and garden philosophy of the 1950s and 1960s. The contraceptive pill created a sexual revolution. Women decided they wanted equal pay and equal say. Divorce laws changed. The rush to take advantage of them showed it wasn't only true love that had been keeping the nation's marriages together. Single-parent families and working wives became as common as traditional couples. All this has created a different childhood for children today.

The red brick childhood of the baby boomers with its inkwells, Saturday afternoon serials and Meccano sets has gone. But we can still share the memory.

CHAPTER ONE

Emoh Ruo (Our Home)

I'm Popeye the Sailor man,
I live in a big caravan.
I eat all the worms,
And spit out the germs.
I'm Popeye the Sailor man.

Life in the Suburbs

Australians have always aspired to be home owners. In the post-war era, with a government-backed building program, the dream began to become reality. Suburbia expanded relentlessly in red brick and fibro. But the sprawl of suburbia, where the vast majority of baby boomers grew up, was not the gadget land of modern suburbia. Some aspects of suburban life were primitive when measured against today's standard of living. Many areas had no kerbing or guttering. Getting the sewer on was a major event in the lives of many suburban children. The dunny man was a real part of life.

You were always scared of redbacks in the outside dunny. It was probably the reason we all had to be dosed up with Laxettes or castor oil.

The sewer seemed like an amazing invention. We knew other people who had it. Actually getting an indoor toilet was like going to live in Hollywood.

The land behind the standard three bedroom suburban house was invariably referred to as the backyard or the yard. It was the focus of domestic life and the focus of life in early childhood. The front yard was the showpiece.

A house to let,
Apply within.
You go out,
I go in.

Dad's weekends were taken up with house and garden.

All the front yards in our street were the same — the fence, the roses, the lawn and then the front garden bed. We moved to Canberra and they had no front fences. Mum was horrified. She thought it was really primitive.

Dad said he was going to fix up the front yard. He got a sleeping Mexican with number forty-seven next to it to screw onto the house. We thought it was the height of sophistication.

Dad got into crazy paving. He did a patio, the driveway, the front path, then the back path. Even Mum thought he was mad.

The Hills Hoist was up the back, next to the chook yard. It was the "whippy" for chasings and we were always in trouble for swinging on it.

My brother wound up the Hills Hoist so high that it fell out.

We had a Kelpie that held onto the Hills Hoist with his teeth. We'd swing him round and round. We had to prise him off.

The back tap played a big part in my early life. Mum was always throwing things down the gully trap and Dad was always digging it out because she'd blocked the drain.

The vegie garden was a terrible hindrance to cricket practice. We had the stumps set up in front of the tomatoes. We batted fabulously because Dad gave us hell if we started knocking the tomatoes around.

Virtually all suburban homes had electricity, but the supply was much less reliable than today. Blackouts were a continuing feature of the baby boomer's life.

Mum was in the backyard hanging out the clothes.

I loved blackouts. We were lucky because we had gas, so we could still cook. We'd sit round the dinner table with candles, feeling really spooked.

We'd always lose the candles — or the matches. Dad would be cursing and saying next time they had to be kept where they were supposed to be kept. They never were.

Whenever there was a blackout, the kids were sent out to see where the streetlights were on and which houses had lights. It didn't make any difference, but it made us feel better that it wasn't just us.

A blackout gave you a real excuse for not having done your homework the next day.

Today, Australians see themselves as part of an urban nation, with urban characteristics and problems. In fact, since the second half of the nineteenth century, Australia has been one of the most urbanised countries in the world. However, until recently, we have seen ourselves as basically country folk at heart. Children of the post-war era, who grew up mostly in the city or the suburbs, saw themselves, in many ways, as essentially rural.

We used to recite Dorothea MacKellar's "I Love a Sunburnt Country". There were trucks roaring up the hill outside the school and smoke billowing out of the factories. Yet, somehow, it felt as if we were part of the bushfires and the brolgas dancing on the plains.

I used to sit in the backyard, on top of a ladder and sing "Advance Australia Fair". I could see all the other backyards, red roofs and Hills Hoists. I felt I was part of this really huge country.

The explorers, the Anzacs, the squatters, the *Country Hour* on the A.B.C. All the things we learnt in primary school made us feel very country, even though we lived in red brick suburbia.

We felt tough compared to the migrant kids from England. They couldn't surf or go on the hot road in bare feet. Their mothers made them wear hats.

Country Kids

City kids enjoyed farm visits.

Many children did, of course, live in the country. Often, they lived under more primitive conditions, without sewerage and without electricity. But undoubtedly, the major difference between country and city children was the isolation of country children.

When we went to stay with our aunty in the city, we felt really shy. I couldn't get over seeing all those people you didn't know. Even the people who lived there didn't know them.

We lived right out, so going into town was a big event. Town was tiny, but it was like the metropolis to us.

I remember going into town and not knowing where to pee. At home, you just went behind a tree.

I did school of the air. I used to fantasise what real school would be like. When I went to boarding school, I hated it.

Daddy is a butcher,
Mummy cuts the meat.
I'm a little Frankfurt,
Running round the street.

The isolation, of course, had its own compensations. Country children may not have been street smart, but they had their own brand of independence.

I was six when I learnt to drive a tractor. It was a big Massey Ferguson. Dad was really proud of me.

Even though there were a lot of farm chores we hated, we knew we could look after ourselves. By the time I was eight I was a great shot with a .22.

I hated the milking. The smell and the mud were awful and the cows were so stupid. It always seemed to be cold and raining.

Dad used to taunt us with the bull. He'd tell us if we didn't behave, he'd set the bull on us. I'm still terrified of bulls.

Summer heat was unrelieved. The only thing was swimming in the dam. If it was a bad summer, there'd be no dam.

We used to go yabbying a lot. You could always catch them, but there was nothing much to do with them. Nobody thought of yabby cocktails.

In Queensland, you were always trying to find a way to kill cane toads. Dad used to blast at them with a shotgun. We kids would go out on the front lawn at night and try and hit them over the house with a golf club.

I hated seeing a sheep being killed. I used to wonder what it had done to deserve it.

My father said it was easier to kill a beast than to grow vegies. We had chops for breakfast, cold meat for lunch and a roast for dinner.

Family Life

Country or city, most children shared a bedroom with their siblings. Families were bigger and houses were smaller. Closer contact didn't always lead to caring and sharing.

My sister was very tidy and I was very messy. It infuriated her that I put all my lolly papers under the bed. But she couldn't quite bring herself to tell on me.

My brother and I had terrible fights. Mum just gave up. There were actually bloodstains down one wall.

We slept three girls to one 12 ft room. There were three beds, one dressing table and one cupboard. The good thing about it was that we told stories all night.

My sister longed for a room of her own. She had locks on everything. I got things out of her desk through the inkwell hole with a pair of tweezers.

I got a box with a padlock for my private things. My brother just broke the box.

Children had their share of household jobs. Some jobs were exclusively for girls, others exclusively for boys.

Mum made me wash out the bath with kerosene. I hated the job and I hated the smell, but she said nothing else was as clean.

We had a fight almost every single night over whose turn it was to wash up and whose turn it was to dry. The aim of the whole thing was to give Mum and Dad a chance to listen to the news in peace. They never did.

We had an old push mower to mow the lawn. We had to do it every week. It was like paradise when Dad finally got a proper Victa.

We had the wood delivered at the beginning of winter. It all had to be chopped. I'd look at it and think I couldn't possibly get through it.

CHAPTER TWO

Fold Your Arms and Sit Up Straight

Dictation, dictation, dictation.
Three sausages went to the station.
One got lost,
One got squashed,
And one had an operation.

ROLL CALL

Popular baby boomer names

Alan
Barbara
Barry
Beverley
Brian
Bruce
Cheryl
Christine
Deirdre
Doug
Elizabeth
Eric
Gary
Gay
Geoffrey
Greg
John
Janet
Kay
Keith
Kevin
Lynette
Margaret
Maureen
Patricia
Ray
Sally
Sandra
Tony

School Rules

Schools today are slightly coy about asserting their muscle and telling students what to do. In the post-war period, schools were still unashamedly authoritarian. There was no question that teachers knew best (except amongst children) and that children should do what they were told. To make this absolutely clear, most schools had a morning line-up as well as a full-blown assembly every week. These rituals reinforced homilies such as 'rules are rules' and 'those that disobey, suffer'.

Marching was a skill taught to children in the belief that it would develop character and self-discipline. For those who were naturally deficient in character, it was often a painful ritual.

I didn't know left from right. We had to stand perfectly still before moving off, so I was scared to even wriggle my fingers to see which was the writing hand. The headmaster would shout, "Right March!" and I'd inevitably lift my left foot. He'd stop the music and we'd have to go through it all again.

I got a report with D's in every subject, but at least it had a comment on the end, "Marching much improved".

There were only three tunes they used for marching — "Turkish Patrol", "Country Gardens" and "Colonel Bogey". The gramophone was in the staffroom and it went out through the loudspeaker. Sometimes, if they left the speaker on, you could hear them quarrelling about which one to play.

Class 5B1 all say 'cheese'!

Left right — or right left?

The use of whistles added to the military atmosphere of schools. The whistle was essential for teachers who could no longer shout.

When the headmaster blew the whistle, you had to stop still and turn and face him. It was like frozen moments, with kids hanging off monkey bars or half way through throwing a ball. If you didn't, the penalty was death.

My mate and I were carrying the milk crates across the playground. There was some scuffle going on and the whistle went. Everybody had to turn and face the teacher. He shouted,

Temperature Conversion Chart

°Farenheit	°Celsius
50	10
60	15.6
70	21.1
80	26.7
90	32.2
100	37.8

School reports could be unnecessarily honest.

BONDI BEACH PUBLIC SCHOOL

Half-Yearly Report

Name *Stephen Townsend (10th in class)*

Class *3 A*

	Marks	Comments
Reading	B⁺	
Composition	B	
Spelling	A⁺	
Writing	B	
Arithmetic	A	
English	A	
Social Studies	A⁺	

Remarks *Stephen is a nuisance sometimes but is still doing very well with less wasted time he could do much better.*

Class Teacher *J. Ryde*

Principal *Dr J. Zvaller*

Parent *B Townsend*

"Everyone drop anything you have in your hands." A heaven sent opportunity — we dropped the milk crates. All the bottles broke and the milk went everywhere. There was a terrible fuss, but it was worth it.

Rule Britannia

Queen and Country played a very important part in education. In spite of the post-war influx of European migrants, Australian children had an all-British education. It was almost with regret that they were told that the British Commonwealth had replaced the British Empire. It was implied that the British had been kind in letting the Indians join the Commonwealth. Education sometimes seemed to be priming pupils to be a future soldier or Red Cross nurse for the Queen. Flags were part of every school's equipment, saluting the flag part of school ritual.

How were your exam questions?
Fine, it was the answers that were hard.

I went through a stage of being intensely patriotic. I desperately wanted to be the boy at the flagpole, but the headmaster hated me.

The headmaster yelled, "I salute my flag!" and we repeated it after him. Simultaneously, the flag was supposed to unfurl. Often it wouldn't unfurl and the headmaster went redder and redder. We stood there in the heat until it learnt to obey orders.

Headmasters were enormously powerful people, known to have canes of extraordinary length and power in their offices. They also controlled the public address system, a sort of big brother spy system, which was one of the major technological and educational advances of the 1950s. There was usually a bench outside their offices on which miscreants sat and waited to be called inside.

This Souvenir of
THE ROYAL VISIT
TO AUSTRALIA
1 9 5 4
is presented to
Judith Russell
of Bexley School School
by
The Commonwealth Government of Australia

If you missed the Queen you could still get the book.

Our headmaster was Scottish and he somehow managed to imply that he was personally deputising on behalf of the Queen. We had the Queen's picture hanging in every room.

The Queen's birthday was celebrated by children as a holiday and usually set off a frenzy of patriotic activity in schools.

We spent hours learning how to draw Union Jacks. I can't remember what all the crosses actually signify. I used to know.

When the Queen actually came to Australia in 1954, it was an enormous event for school children. In Sydney, children were taken to the R.A.S. showground and made to wait for hours until the Queen finally appeared. The children waved their flags as the Queen drove through. In other cities and in country centres, the scenario was repeated again and again.

There were thousands of kids and we were dropping off like flies, standing in the heat, with nothing to eat or drink. We were so buoyed up that we were finally going to see HER. We had flags we'd coloured in with crayon and it was so hot that the colours ran. Finally she came. Nobody would say they didn't like it, but it was disappointing. She looked like an ordinary woman. She wasn't even wearing a crown.

Special Days

Anzac Day and Remembrance Day were also big events on the patriotic calendar and children had to learn songs such as the 'British Grenadier' and the 'Recessional', as well as brushing up on marching. The Anzac landing was explained, every year, in long and boring detail.

Latin is a language
As dead as dead can be.
First it killed the Romans
And now it's killing me.

I'll never forget the first Anzac Day I went to with my Dad. The march was pretty much as I expected but then we went to the pub, where I had to wait outside. Then there was a two-up game. I'd never seen anything like it and my Dad was in there with the best of them. It was very exciting. He turned round and said, "This is the real Anzac son." I never felt the same about the dawn landing.

Dad had fought in the war and he used to come to school on Anzac Day and talk about the Battle of the Coral Sea. I got terribly embarrassed. I was envious of kids whose fathers had died in the war.

Currency

12 pence = 1 shilling
20 shillings = 1 pound
240 pence = 1 pound
1 pound and 1 shilling = 1 guinea

School Milk

During World War II, it had been discovered that the nutritional standards of many Australian soldiers were very poor. In the post-war era, schools took it upon themselves to remedy this by forcing every child to drink a quarter of a pint of milk every day. Free milk was symbolic of post-war reconstruction, along with Baby Health Centres and immunisation programs.

One kid got the bright idea of bringing chocolate Quik to put in his milk. Fantastic! Next day it was announced at assembly that milk was to be drunk straight. No Quik!

I can remember the milk crates standing in the sun outside the classroom. When we got out to playlunch, the teacher would give out striped paper straws, red for girls, blue for boys. It always tasted awful. Some of the kids just drank it straight down and went off to play. The teacher stood over the rest of us, making sure we finished. The straw always got soggy.

The Best Days of Our Lives

Education was far more standardised than today. There was no such thing as the open classroom. From kindergarten, children sat at desks, boys on one side of the room, girls on the other. The ultimate punishment was to have to sit next to a member of the opposite sex.

CLASS CAPTAIN

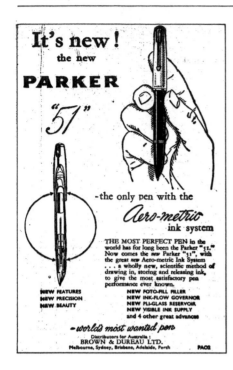

It had to be a Parker pen.

What was wrong with the cross-eyed teacher?
He had trouble with his pupils.

In kindergarten we grew wheat in cotton wool, onions in milk bottles and made potato prints and did finger painting. Transition was where the heavy stuff started.

We had green Feltex mats for our afternoon sleep. They had a complicated marbled pattern and they really made your skin itch. You couldn't scratch because the teacher had a ruler and would take a swipe at anyone who "wasn't sleeping properly". It was hardly relaxing.

First class you had pencils and you learned printing with the bat and ball method. Then you graduated to running writing and slope cards. Third class was big time — you got ink and pens. They'd mix up the ink every Monday and pour it into the inkwells which sat in a hole in the desk. It was always gritty towards the end of the week.

I learnt to read out of the "Janet and John" books which were all about catching buses in London. It didn't do you much good to read, because we didn't have a school library.

We did a lot of grammar, even in primary — adjectival phrases, pluperfect tenses, parsing sentences. We had competitions to see who could parse fastest and we'd all be there with our hands up, screaming "Sir, Sir, Sir!" I couldn't do it to save my life now, but it seemed quite exciting at the time.

A fountain pen was the status symbol. It came in a velvet lined case and had a rubber tube you filled with ink — Quink Ink, not the ordinary school ink. You had to be careful you didn't twist the nibs because they were expensive. The best thing was that you could release a lot of ink onto the nib and then flick it halfway across the classroom.

No way could you use a biro — they were lower class.

Geography was filling in the red bits on the map of the world for the British Commonwealth. History was much the same and then we had social studies which was the same too.

Poetry was terribly important. And the main thing was to learn it off by heart. We did a lot of good rousing sort of poetry — Banjo Paterson stuff. The only thing that detracted from it was that you got caned if you didn't know the week's piece by Friday.

We did nature study on Fridays. Sometimes we pressed flowers and sometimes we traced round gum leaves. Because it was nature study, we did it outside.

Cultural Cringe

Culture was not forgotten. There was a disturbing realisation by the authorities after World War II that Australia was somehow lacking in 'culture'. Unfortunately, the education system seemed at a loss to know exactly how to broaden the cultural outlook of pupils. Folk dancing, which quickly degenerated into American square dancing, was part of an early multicultural thrust. Eurythmics, in some schools, provided an unpopular alternative to the traditional competitive sports. Recorders were introduced on the theory that they were a musical instrument every child could play. This theory was not entirely true. Percussion bands and school choirs remained popular.

One of the boys in our school was American and he actually admitted he liked folk dancing. It finished him. It was as bad as admitting you liked girls.

You were partnered off for a whole term to one partner. I got a boy I hated because he had red hair. I told everyone he had smelly hands.

I was the conductor of the percussion. I liked being in charge, but the rest of them wouldn't take any notice. You conducted by standing on a chair and pointing. It was terribly frustrating. I pointed at the cymbals but they wouldn't stop. The girl with the triangle was staring at the ceiling so it didn't do any good to point. Afterwards, I had a terrible feeling it had been my fault.

We did a lot of singing. Songs like "The Ashgrove", "Loch Lomond" and "John Peel". If you couldn't sing in tune, you had to move your mouth in time.

We used to practise "voice speaking" on Friday afternoons. It was for eisteddfods. The whole class would have to go through enunciating the vowels — a, e, i, o, u — in very plummy tones.

IMPERIAL UNITS

Length

12 inches = 1 foot
3 feet = 1 yard
1760 yards = 1 mile

1 rod, perch or pole = 16½ feet
  or 5½ yards
100 links = 1 chain
1 chain = 66 feet
30¼ yards = 1 perch
80 chains = 1 mile

Area

144 square inches = 1 square foot
9 square feet = 1 square yard
4840 square yards = 1 acre
640 square acres = 1 square mile

Volume

20 fluid ounces = 1 pint
4 gills = 1 pint
2 pints = 1 quart
4 quarts = 1 gallon

Weight

16 ounces = 1 pound
14 pounds = 1 stone
8 stone = 1 hundredweight
20 hundredweight = 1 ton

Everyone start when I say 'three'.

Then the best kid would get up and recite "The Owl and the Pussycat". After "voice speaking" was over, we went back to ordinary old speaking — the yeahs, you knows, thems, youse.

Drama was a big thing. There was the organisation called the British Drama League. The headmaster got enthused and we put on a play for the first and last time. My little brother was in the chorus line of animals up the front. He got so excited by the applause that he started taking off all his clothes. They couldn't get to him without disrupting the whole thing. The parents thought they'd never seen anything so hysterically funny in their whole lives, but the headmaster was fuming.

My mother hated recorders. "If you're going to play those damn whistles," she'd say, "Play them down the paddock."

Craftwork was embraced as another way of broadening education beyond the three R's. As well as the traditional crafts — sewing for girls, woodwork for boys — schools also introduced basket weaving, papier-mâché, pottery and weaving.

No more English, no more French,
No more sitting on a hard wood bench.
No more spelling, no more sums,
No more whacks across our bums.

We had to stick samples of all the different stitches into a book with paste. I ate a great deal of Perkins Paste.

We had to make a pair of pants out of green headcloth. I could not understand what I was doing and I kept sewing the legs together. I was eventually banned from sewing for speeding on the sewing machine.

When you were in kindergarten and made pottery ashtrays, you felt pretty good about it. By the time you were fifteen and making metal sugar scoops for your mother, you knew they were crummy.

I desperately wanted to give my Mum the wastepaper basket I was making for Christmas. But it kept veering off to one side. Finally, I finished it and lacquered it so it'd stand up straight. Then one morning Dad stepped on it. It fell over and all the chips of lacquer went everywhere. I felt really hurt when I heard Mum and Dad laughing about it.

School of Hard Knocks

Of course, as in schools today, education came as much from experiences in the playground as from the formal learning in the classroom.

They were always daring you to run through the girls' toilets. It took me until I was ten to get the courage to do it. I was really disappointed. I thought it would be full of naked women or something.

Running through the girls' toilets was the most incredible dare. And thrilling — all those little girls screaming!

The playground was divided up — this bit for infants, this bit for fifth class, but the biggest division was between boys and girls. You'd throw the ball over, by "mistake" and hassle the girls as you went to get it.

On rainy days, we had to eat lunch in the shelter shed. The teachers sent classes to different parts, but inside, it was a jungle. Your position in the shelter shed really let you know where you ranked at school.

You'd squeeze in and get to sit on the end of the seat, then some kid would push from the other end. You'd be back on the concrete floor or have to sit on someone's lap.

The Paddle Pop beat the sandwiches!

My worst experience of school was being hung up on the coat rack by my skirt.

You'd have your Vegemite sandwich in a brown paper bag. On hot days, it'd curl round the edges. Then you'd have a frozen drink in a plastic bottle. You wrote your name on a piece of Elastoplast and stuck it on.

The snag about lunchtime was that you had to eat lunch. I can still remember the smell of a Vegemite sandwich in a Globite suitcase, with an apple that had brown bits.

The monkey bars were the thing. A group of us would get possession. You couldn't stop swinging on them for a moment because someone else would grab them from you. I developed awful calluses on my hands.

We had five minutes at the end of lunch for picking up papers. From being these high-speed monsters, we'd degenerate into kids too exhausted to do anything.

You'd race up after school to the bus stop to make sure you got a seat at the back of the bus. When you were little, it seemed like everything happened at the back of the bus, kissing and smoking and the big financial deals.

We used to despise the kids who sat down on the train. You'd stand right next to the open door, talking to girls. The "in" crowd were the ones in danger of imminent death.

I don't know why, but we persecuted the bus drivers. They were always big, fat, sweaty guys and you'd refuse to show them your bus pass or to sit down. They'd be threatening to take your name or report you to the school or throw you off the bus. Nothing ever happened. I don't know why we hated them so much.

School, of course, spilled over into other activities. School was the centre for sport and games, formal and informal. It was the place where many baby boomers learnt about sex, again, both formally and informally. It was the major meeting place of the era. Its activities, rules and restrictions influenced many other spheres of life.

CHAPTER THREE

Getting Organised

I am a Girl Guide dressed in blue.
These are the actions I must do:
Stand at ease, bend your knees,
Salute to the King, bow to the Queen.
Never turn your back on the Union Jack!

Signing Up

Mothers were people who spent their time doing housework, shopping and cooking. In the context of their constant activity, the children were, for the most part, a nuisance. Apart from the obligatory afternoon tea after school and homework after dinner, children were left fairly free. However, it was thought to be a 'good thing', if they belonged to or participated in various community organisations and activities. Chief amongst these were the Boy Scouts and the Girl Guides and their junior counterparts, Cubs and Brownies.

I loved Cubs. Every kid in the neighbourhood went and I thought it was something you had to go to, like school. It surprised me they were nice.

We had a dreadful Akela. Her basic problem was that she hated kids. We used to give her a hard time because we knew she had her eye on the Scout master.

My mother bought the Brownie uniform, even the special shoes and socks and the badge with the little elf on it. I went once and then I jacked up. I only wanted the badge.

We used to spend a lot of time being elves and leprechauns and dancing round in circles with imaginary toadstools. We'd sing a song like this one:
    "We are the Irish leprechauns,
    Guiding strangers when forlorn."

My very first Brownie certificate.

It was an effort getting there. You had to polish the badges, have your shoes shined and the scarf straight. We all had to hold out our hands so the Brown Owl could make sure we had clean fingernails.

I wrote in my diary: "Today I joined the Brownies. It was the proudest moment of my life."

When Lady Baden-Powell came out from England to visit us, it was like royalty. I was chosen to appear with her on a daytime television program. They interviewed her and then I had to demonstrate one of the Brownie skills. I'd been practising for weeks. I folded a pair of socks.

I loved the badges. I got one for morse code, one for first aid and a couple of others. The thing I enjoyed most was the knots. I can still do a clove hitch and a good reef knot.

I got my first experience of cooking at a Scout camp. I heard you made stew by chucking everything into it and boiling it up. The baked beans and the beetroot went in. No-one ate it.

I desperately wanted to go to a jamboree. I hassled Mum until she let me go. We couldn't afford it for years, but I hung in at Scouts because she was trying to get the money together. When I finally did go, I was too old.

The jamborees were a survival test. It was every man for himself and may the best man win. It was pouring rain and we were huddled in the tent. A bloke poked his head in and said there was hot food up at the mess. There wasn't and when we came back, our tent was gone.

You heard terrible things about the Scouts. We Guides regarded ourselves as far more serious, responsible and mature. I don't think we had as much fun.

Other organisations such as the Boys' Brigade and the Girls' Brigade were as strictly segregated into boys and girls, as obsessive about uniforms and as patriotic and God-fearing as Scouts and Guides. As a church-based organisation, there was a more generous dose of religion. Police Boys Clubs, by contrast, tended to concentrate heavily on physical activity.

The Boys' Brigade was great for inner city kids like us. We did all sorts of very heavy physical stuff which kept us very busy. Getting into trouble was about the only other thing we could have done.

I loved the Boys' Brigade because we had a forage cap and a silver badge. I pretended it was the Air Force.

Gymnastics was an important part of the girls' activity. I felt terrific the first time I learnt how to do a cartwheel. But then they told me I couldn't go into the display because my headstand was wobbly. I never went back.

Police Boys was great. You learnt boxing and judo. There were lots of tough kids who came. The cops threatened to nick them if they didn't.

The basics of survival at Scout camp.

The human pyramid.

Nature Lovers

In the post-war years, ecology had not yet risen to become a political movement. It still meant counting starfish at high tide. There was no such species as an environmentalist. However the children of the post-war era were not immune to nature. Dorothea Mackellar's 'I Love a Sunburnt Country' was learnt off by heart by a generation of schoolchildren. There were numerous organisations to encourage children to protect plants and animals.

Plant the tree and watch it grow.

We always had Arbor Day. We planted a tree every year in the same place. Every year it died.

We always had a big project for Arbor Day about soil erosion and the danger it posed to Australia. But we weren't allowed to have trees in the playground because they'd ruin the ashphalt.

We'd buy the badge for the Gould League of bird lovers every year. They were very pretty badges and they cost two shillings each. We were told it was for a very worthy cause, but we never knew what they did with the money.

My Gould League badge was confiscated for shooting sparrows with a slingshot.

We weren't allowed to colour in galahs in the Gould League magazine until we'd done magpies properly.

Those Less Fortunate

There were also those 'less fortunate than ourselves'. Some of the less fortunate were looked after by money raised through school or church organisations. The junior Red Cross claimed almost universal membership of primary school children. In some schools, sympathy for 'our dumb friends' evoked waves of activity to assist the R.S.P.C.A. In NSW, Stewart House gave deprived children a seaside holiday. Throughout Australia, children were called on to support Legacy, to help the children of war widows.

The worst thing I ever did was sell toffees for the Red Cross and then keep all the money.

The least popular girl in the school had lost her father in the war. Legacy never got much until she left.

We used to get Red Cross badges in the shape of native animals. The teacher said we couldn't buy one unless we had a totally sincere intention to come to the meetings every week. But by the end of the year, there was never anyone at the Red Cross meetings.

Junior Red Cross rally for Anzac Day.

I made a baby's nightie and gave it to the Red Cross. I was mortified when the teacher told me they couldn't take it because it was too grubby.

A man from the R.S.P.C.A. came and told us about being kind to animals. I got the impression they went around patting dogs.

We had to bring money for charity every Friday. If you put in more than a shilling, your name got put in a book. They told us when the book was full, they sent it to the Queen. She read it after she'd had her tea, sitting next to the fire.

A Touch of Class

Self-improvement was another important part of growing up. Piano lessons were a symbol of middle-class affluence and a sign of culture. In addition, many girls 'did' ballet. The less graceful did physical culture. Voice production was thought to add 'polish' to the otherwise unpolished child.

I came home one day to find a Palings piano in the lounge room. Mum told me that Dad had decided not to get a car so I'd be able to have lessons. It did something to my mind. I couldn't play a note.

The piano lessons were horrendous. Like all piano teachers, my teacher was very old and had a lot of wrinkles. She told me I'd never pass my exams at the rate I was going. I didn't want to pass my exams.

I loved piano, but I hated the concerts. Every child in my year played "Dance of the Gnomes" or "Für Elise" and then the parents clapped. It really put you off.

I was always scared my parents would embarrass me at the Christmas ballet concert. Dad threatened to give me a standing ovation. I could tell from Mum's face that she wanted to rush onto the stage and adjust my costume.

All I wanted to do was dance like Margot Fonteyn. I couldn't understand why I had to bother with first position and second position.

On her points! Every little girl's dream.

I loved ballet lessons. The best thing was having a tutu at the end of the year concert.

I was what they called a "big girl". There was this awful thud, thud, thud when I jumped. The whole hall seemed to reverberate.

At physical culture, we had to line up in teams. The teacher would call out "CO—mmence". We'd all move forward in a special routine of steps, hops and runs.

The teacher told me that if you did a forward roll wrongly, you could break your neck and end up a cripple. I didn't want to do a forward roll.

My elocution teacher would say, "I want you to sound natural, my dears." She had an incredibly plummy voice. We'd all giggle and as punishment, she'd make us recite "The Owl and the Pussycat".

CHAPTER FOUR

But They're Starving in India

Mabel, Mabel.
Set the table.
Don't forget
The salt and pepper.

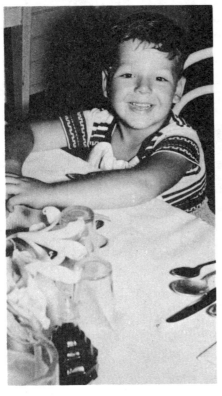

Sometimes the anticipation was better than the meal.

Food Glorious Food

As a nation of primary producers, Australians have always prided themselves on the quality of their food. As a result, Australian children have been inculcated with the idea of gratitude for their food. In the immediate post-war period, this gratitude was highlighted in many families, by saving dripping for hungry British children — the 'Fat for Britain' drive. In the interests of continuing gratitude, Australian children were never told that most of the fat collected was unusable. It was used to make soap, of which the British had too much anyway.

Boiled sausages. They were grey, full of liquid fat. I can't imagine how Mum thought of them.

It's a wonder we didn't die of heart disease. We used to have a meat loaf made of sausage mince. First time round it was cooked in a tin. Then, until we finished it, Mum would fry the slices. I'd get it out of the fridge for her. It would be covered in hard white fat. I'd think I couldn't eat it again. But we had to.

'Rare' was an unknown word in relation to meat. A pink lamb chop or a steak with any juice left was regarded as unhygienic by the Australian housewife. Underdone pork was likely to be teeming with hydatids and was left in the oven until it was regulation brown. But the worst meals were those where the cooks experimented.

36

The curries from the left-over roast . . . Keen's curry powder and bits of apple and sultana floating round in it.

Fricassee of neck chops. It came with white sauce, parsley and mashed carrots.

Mum was overgenerous with the Gravox. If she was feeling daring, she'd throw in a spoonful of Bonox too.

Our meals were recycled. The fridge was full of plastic containers with old bits of stew or vegetables being saved for bubble and squeak. Thank God I'd left home by the time Glad Wrap was invented.

Vegetables were thoroughly cooked first time round. They were then recycled as bubble and squeak or in vegetable salads. Food had be fresh when it was bought, but this freshness was taken care of by the indefatigable Australian housewife.

Three vegies were standard. Carrots — sliced, cubed or mashed. A dash of bi-carb. Mashed potatoes or boiled potatoes. They were cooked so long they were grey. And peas. Nanna never used to say anything but she'd always make this awful choking sound if Mum didn't cook them long enough.

Mum would talk about having a lovely fresh salad for Saturday lunch. The only fresh stuff were the tomatoes and lettuce. Then Mum added tinned pineapple, cocktail onions, tinned asparagus, hard boiled eggs, tinned beetroot and tinned baked beans, with processed cheese and tinned ham. The mayonnaise was made of sweetened condensed milk and Cornwall's malt vinegar. When guests came, we bought olives and called it a continental salad.

Chokos were tasteless and slightly slimy, but they were free because of the vine over the dunny. Dad's tomatoes might fail, but never the chokos. When the crop finished, there was choko chutney, choko jam and choko preserves.

I'd sit with the cabbage in front of me, not knowing how I could eat it. Squash was another one. It was very appropriate that it was called squash.

Curry was a useful camouflage.

Keen's Curry makes good cooks better!

Keen's Curry has wonderful ways with all kinds of foods. Used in the right amount it makes delicious curries exactly to your taste — mild, medium or hot. Its delicate blend and true Indian flavour add a new subtlety to many dishes. Try a little today in your soup, stew, casserole or summer salad.

GOES FURTHER!

KEEN'S CURRY

FINEST QUALITY CURRY PO

TRUE INDIAN FLAVOUR!

Keen's Curry

MAKES MILD, MEDIUM OR HOT CURRIES

Made by the manufacturers of Keen's Mustard

T'was in a restaurant they met,
Romeo and Juliet.
He found he couldn't pay the
*   debt,*
So Romeo'd what Juliet.

What did the little girl say to her
*   father when he fell in the*
*   river?*
Paddle Pop!

Preserving was a major activity. We'd buy cases of whatever was in season — sometimes from the side of the road, but sometimes blokes would sell door to door. Mum and Dad used Fowler's Vacola jars. They had to be sterilised otherwise you were in danger of the dreaded tomaine poisoning. The most exciting bit was when the pressure cooker exploded and sprayed whatever it was all over the roof. It was like waiting for the whale to spout.

Keeping Us Supplied

Supermarkets did not come to Australia until the late 1950s. For some time after their arrival, individual shops and shopkeepers continued to play a far more important role than they do today.

You could tell a grocer. He was the bloke with the pencil behind his ear.

The grocer doled out flour, sugar and a pat of butter. He wrapped everything himself. If it was too much to fit in the string bag, he'd send the boy round later. I'd always be tugging at Mum to get her to buy broken biscuits. They were threepence a bag.

We used to take all the old newspapers up to the butcher. There were always people waiting on a bench on one side of the shop. The carcasses were hanging in the shop and the butcher cut everything up in front of you. It was all rather grisly. Our order was always the same — two pounds of tripe, one good liver, three kidneys, an H bone roast, neck chops, not too tough, and a bone for the dog.

The ice man delivered ice for the ice chest. He'd chop a block off with the pick and we kids would get the slivers. We finally got the fridge, a "Silent Night". Even though it only ran on kero, it was really, really cold.

The milko was my hero. He was an enormous, strong bloke and he'd jump the fences with 10 gallon pitchers of milk in each hand. You'd leave your jug at the back door and he'd fill it up, and then jump over the fence to the neighbours. One day, his foot caught on the pickets and he went head over heels. It was very dramatic with milk and blood all over the backyard.

Women probably did run off with the milkman. They were always big and strong and amiable.

The rabbito was a little shifty guy, who went round yelling "Rabbito! Rabbito!". He was pretty quick and Mum would send us running after him. We'd say we couldn't catch him because we hated rabbit stew.

The bread man left the order in the breadbox at the front gate, and the kids were sent down to get it. The high top loaf was the best. It split in half. One side was concave and the other side bulged out. It was still warm and you started pulling off strips, until both sides were hollowed out. By the time you got home, there was just a crusty shell.

The fruit and vegetable man who delivered to the house was Chinese, but the people up at the greengrocers were Italian. They were the only foreigners I knew when I was growing up. But we never ate anything foreign like zucchini or capsicum.

Mind your Manners

Australian mealtimes have become increasingly informal. Until the 1960s, there was very little prepackaged or fast food available. All meals were a grand production, exclusively prepared by Mum. It's little wonder she demanded clean plates and gratitude.

Breakfast kept coming at you. Toast, Lackensteins' marmalade in a tin, Kellogg's Corn Flakes, bacon, kidneys, rubbery scrambled eggs, tinned fruit. When it was time for school, you were stupefied by food.

Whenever there was a new packet of cereal, we had a near riot at breakfast. We scrambled for the card or the plastic car or the Superman figure at the bottom. Even worse were the cutouts on the packets. Laying claim to those was very tricky.

We had the table set at every meal. Mum used to go mad if there was a spot on the tablecloth, so we hid them with the salt and pepper and the serviettes. Keeping your serviette clean was an art in itself. If you got food on your face or your hands, you were a dirty child. If you got it on your dress, you were

What sort of jam can't you eat?
Traffic jam!

What did one strawberry say to the other strawberry?
If it weren't for you we wouldn't be in this jam.

If all the world were paper,
And all the sea were ink,
And all the trees were bread and cheese,
What on earth would we drink?

Ice-cream and jelly
A punch in the belly.

I scream
You scream
We all scream
For ice-cream.

Wash the dishes
Dry the dishes
Turn the dishes over.

Outside meals were less formal.

filthy. The serviettes were supposed to last a week. Every meal they were put away in rings and then brought out again.

Farting at the table was a terrible crime. The actual word was never used. It was, "Who did that?" Nobody ever owned up, but someone was always sent off in disgrace, as if the smell would go with them. If there were guests, it was ignored.

Eating up every scrap was mandatory. My mother was the original standover merchant.

Thank God for the dog. It would eat anything — cabbage, tripe or blancmange — whatever you whipped under the table. After dinner, it got the scraps too.

The best meals we had were on Sunday nights — Heinz spaghetti in tomato sauce round the Kero Fyreside. We thought it was the height of sophistication.

We'd have Welsh rarebit or spaghetti with Kia-Ora canned mince on a rainy Saturday. We had it at the kitchen table, without the grown-ups. We did the most incredibly obscene things with the spaghetti.

Jaffle irons came in — not the electric ones, but the old round ones you held over a flame. Mum filled the jaffles with rice, flavoured with Heinz tomato sauce. They were fantastic!

I had a bet with my brother that I could eat a whole jar of Vegemite. I did a very impressive projectile vomit onto the opposite wall.

We felt sorry for kids who had Marmite instead of Vegemite. It was akin to having a runny nose or being smelly.

I can't remember eating out at a restaurant as a child and I doubt my parents ever did either. It didn't happen.

The first take-away was Chinese. You'd go down to the Chinese restaurant with your own saucepan and they'd fill it up. We always had sweet and sour. It was full of pineapple pieces and peas, in a bright orange sauce. If you got another dish, they put a bit of greaseproof paper in between.

Even More Food . . .

In the epicurean desert of Australian cuisine, puddings, cakes and sweets were the culinary highlight for many Australian children. But they too, had their peculiarities.

I always thought the skin was the best part of the rice pudding, like the cream at the top of the milk.

Mum used to make flummery, which was like rubber. Even when you sucked it, it didn't dissolve.

Blancmange came in chocolate, strawberry and other flavours, but basically, they all tasted the same. We had it with jelly, which was either all sloppy or rubbery at the bottom.

We're happy little Vegemites,
As bright, as bright can be,
We all adore our Vegemite,
For breakfast, lunch and tea.

I never knew the difference between blancmange and junket.

Mum used to make ice-cream with condensed milk and evaporated milk in little tin trays. She got it out of the fridge about 3 o'clock and whipped it up like mad. It still settled into two layers. It left a fuzzy feeling on the top of your mouth.

Sago pudding, Yuk! It tasted like stewed gravel.

Tinned fruit or preserved fruit and ice-cream. If there were guests, Mum would put a triangular wafer and a cherry on top. She called it American dessert.

Trifle was a very sophisticated dessert. It was old bits of sponge with a dash of sherry, custard, jelly and tinned fruit.

The best desserts were when we went to the country. We'd go out and get blackberries and have them with that day's cream.

After dinner the kids would have to clear the table and wash up and dry. Mum and Dad would listen to the A.B.C. news at 7 o'clock with their coffee. Actually, it wasn't coffee. It was Bushell's coffee and chicory mixture out of a bottle, but it seemed more sophisticated than a cup of tea.

These considerable quantities of food were shopped for, prepared and cooked by mothers. Mum's job, over and above all else — keeping the sheets Persil white and cleaning the house — was the provision of food. As well as breakfast, lunch and tea, there were substantial morning and afternoon teas.

Before I started school, my mother made me a morning tea of sliced banana with milk and sugar. Every day at ten. It never varied.

We had Kraft cheese on a Vita-Weet or a Sao at morning tea. If the cheese got stuck on the top of your mouth, it was impossible to break the suction. You had to wait until it melted.

Mum made a batch of Anzac biscuits every week. Someone would always come in for morning tea. The women talked about all sorts of amazing things — sex and husbands and strange illnesses. On the weekends it was really dull because the men came and talked about gardening and seed catalogues.

We always had afternoon tea when we got home from school. A glass of milk and cake of some kind — date loaf, tea cake or yeast buns.

Mum either gave us Anzac biscuits for afternoon tea or those biscuits with dates — squashed fly biscuits we used to call them.

Sweets and Treats

However not all food came from the bosom of the family. Pocket money and treats allowed some food to be independently acquired, usually in the form of lollies.

The fellow at the corner shop always behaved as if he was very put upon by the kids in the shop. You'd agonise over whether to get a halfpenny's worth of Clinkers or splurge on Cobbers. He must have done all right out of us because half his display was lollies.

I got sixpence pocket money and I used to agonise over how to spend it. You could buy a comic, but gratification from the lolly shop was faster. You could wait and get a chocolate Paddle Pop from the ice-cream man. He came round in a ute. It had dry ice in the back. He hung his arm out the window and rang a bell.

At school on Red Cross days you could buy toffees in paper. They pulled your fillings out.

The Easter show was the place to get lollies. My sister used to save her sample bags for months. I'd be furious because I ate mine at the bus stop on the way home. I'd be sick as well.

I always felt terrible after the Easter show. My mother was unsympathetic. She claimed I'd overheated my blood, eating all those sweets.

Apart from Paddle Pops and Icey Poles, there weren't many ice-creams. "Hearts" were a really big treat and so were

TRIP DOWN LOLLY LANE

Cobbers
Musk sticks
Slate sticks
Conversation lollies
Coconut quivers
Choo Choo Bars
Licorice aniseed chews
Sugar pigs
SOS lollies
Licorice straps
Sherberts
Rainbow balls
Soldiers' hats
Honey bears
Rosy apples
Minties
Pez dispensers
Nigger Boy licorice
Fantales
Maltezes
Violet Crumble bars
Aniseed balls
Jaffas
Ice mints
Q-bans
Bobbies
Curls

Be careful of your good clothes.

ANZAC BISCUITS

Ingredients

1 cup rolled oats
¾ cup of coconut
1 cup of flour
1½ teaspoons of bicarbonate of
*   soda*
2 tablespoons of boiling water
1 cup of sugar
½ cup of butter
1 tablespoon of golden syrup

Mix oats, flour, sugar and
coconut. Melt butter and golden
syrup. Mix soda with the boiling
water and add to melted butter
and syrup. Add to dry
ingredients. Place tablespoons of
mixture on a greased tin. Bake in
a slow oven for twenty minutes.

Eskimo Pies. You could buy wafers or cones and it was always hard to decide which was better value. The good thing about ice-cream was that your mother thought it was healthy. That was from "Peters — Health Food of the Nation".

The man who delivered the soft drinks was usually the man who made them. That's why Coke was such a big thing. It was glamorous and American.

I loved my grandmother desperately. She used to wear one of those big cardigans. She always had Q-ban sweets in the pockets.

Flavoured straws were lined with chocolate or strawberry and you got the flavour as the milk came up. They took them off the market because they bred some dreadful germ.

The slate pencil lollies were incredibly hard. You could suck them to a fine point and stab people.

I used to love that Lonnie Donnigan song, "Does Your Chewing Gum Lose its Flavour on the Bedpost Overnight?" I had a better idea. I'd store mine at night in a glass of water, sweetened with sugar. In the morning, I'd take it out and drink the sugary water. My record was fourteen days.

You could go to the fish and chip shop and get them to scrape out all the bits floating round in the oil. They cost a penny and I thought they were better than the real thing.

The little Nestlés chocolates cost threepence. They had the birds in the nests on front in gold. They tasted better than the big blocks.

CHAPTER FIVE

And a Clean Pair of Underpants

Giddy giddy gout,
Your shirt's hanging out.
Ten miles in,
Ten miles out.

The Clothes We Wore

Children's fashion is a relatively recent development. Babies, of course, have always needed special clothing, but for many years, children's clothes were simply scaled down versions of adult clothes. In the post-war period, with the lifting of clothing rationing imposed during the war, clothes became more extravagant. This had little effect on the style of children's clothes. The average child's wardrobe remained relatively modest, consisting largely of homemade or hand-me-downs. Each child had three sets of clothes — play clothes, school clothes and the 'going out' outfit. Warm, sensible clothing was the keynote.

The first piece of clothing I remember was a sleep suit. It was less a piece of clothing than a method of incarceration. Where the legs should have been, was a big bag. It was impossible to take it off. I had to let myself over the side of the cot and drag myself out of the house and down the drive.

Babies had flannel. My baby brother had flannel singlets, flannel nappies, English flannel pilchers and flannel jackets. They let him out when he was about two.

My grandmother sent clothes from England. They were regarded as very superior. She sent a blue tweed coat with a little velvet collar which arrived in midsummer. I insisted on wearing it on the tram and nearly had heatstroke.

45

Dressed in British best.

I had great trouble dressing myself. My singlets did up with bows. There were buttons down the back of my dresses, buttons on the cuffs and a sash that had to be tied in a bow at the back. I got sick of it and I tied my sash at the front.

Cardigans were the worst. Not only was it a dreadful word to say, but they seemed to have a hundred buttons. When you got to the last button and you'd run out of button holes, you realised you hadn't matched the button and the hole at the top.

The relief when zippered flies came in! You'd be dying to go and you'd have to unbutton your fly in a hurry.

We were city kids, but we all wore jodhpurs in winter to play in. It was a sort of Australian thing. We would have all been living in the country if we hadn't lived in the city for the last three generations.

The raincoats were like storm gear. They were black and rubbery and lined with some sort of canvas. Once the canvas got wet, it never, ever dried. They smelt like an old lunch.

We always wore knee high gumboots. Mum was strict about not getting them wet inside. Of course we did. The moment the gutters started running we took off our gumboots and went barefoot. We used to float the gumboots down the gutters.

It was a wonderful feeling to get to school and take off your shoes and socks to dry out in front of the Cosi heater.

Underclothes were terrible. We had poplin bloomers that went sort of grey and raggy. Then the cotton ones came in, but they went baggy after you'd worn them a couple of times. Sometimes there was lace on the singlets, but it always unravelled.

Mum used to dry my underpants in the oven on newspaper. I'd go off to school, wearing hot, damp Y-fronts, smelling of wet newspaper.

I had a pair of tartan slippers with a zip and a matching tartan dressing-gown. Unfortunately, my pyjamas were striped flannel.

Girls' Gear

Going out clothes for girls had enough glamour and style to capture the imagination. Sashes, Peter Pan collars, puffed sleeves, boleros, patent-leather shoes, twin-sets, sausage curls, ringlets and ribbons were the order of the day. For boys, it was a drab school suit or a clean white shirt and grey trousers.

I really wanted a nylon dress when they came in. The skirts stuck out the way cotton ones were supposed to, but never did. Nylon felt like plastic which was an added attraction. The kid over the road got one. White, with red spots, red smocking and a big red sash. She wore it with patent-leather shoes, white socks and red bows in her hair. I never forgave her.

We used to run around holding our skirts out. We thought it looked cute. It was wonderful to have one with a full skirt that would twirl around with you.

Mum made our clothes to save money. She bought a length of pink linen and made us all pink linen dresses. The dresses were taken in, let out and let down. Finally, I, the youngest, was the last owner of the last pink linen dress. I insisted on wearing it to school and I sat on a cherry. I ran straight home, but Mum couldn't get the stain out. It was like breaking a family heirloom.

I desperately wanted a pink twin-set, but Mum always knitted me a jumper in sensible cable stitch navy blue. I wore it with a calico bodice and a tartan skirt, which was let down every year.

One birthday, one of my aunties gave me a pale pink orlon twin-set with pearl buttons. No-one had ever heard of orlon, let alone owned a pink orlon twin-set.

The finishing touch was a string of pearls and one of those solid gold bracelets. I was really jealous of my friend because her mother got her a bracelet when she was a baby and she couldn't get it off.

When we went out my sisters wore blue vyella dresses and boleros. I was in my school suit, with the school crest on the pocket.

CLOTHES

Party dress with sash
Puff sleeves
Smocked frocks
Vyella dresses
Jodhpurs
Peter Pan collars
Head bands
Bloomers
Braces
Yakka overalls
Red Robin socks
Patent leather shoes
Flannel shirts
Baby doll pyjamas
Ski pyjamas
Chenille dressing gowns
Tartan dressing gowns
Tartan slippers
Stamina suits
Gumboots
Deerstalker hats
School shoes
Sandshoes
Gym tunics
Box pleated tunics
Duffle coats
Cardigans
Pleated skirts
Court shoes
Twin sets
Jerkins
Milkmaid blouse
Jeans
Kookie jackets
Mini skirts
Stretch pants
Car coats
Bermuda shorts
Rope petticoats
Fluorescent socks
Winkle pickers
Flares

When you're at the tub,
Think of me with every rub.
Though the suds are ever so hot,
Lather your clothes and forget-
*   me-not.*

Shoe Time

Shoes were a major part of clothing expenditure. Considerable thought was put into their purchase and care. Like clothes, they were handed down, repaired and recycled.

There were foot X-ray machines in all the shops. You looked at the bones in your feet while you were waiting to get fitted. The sales assistant looked down one side and you looked down the other. It's a wonder we haven't all got foot cancer.

I can remember the smell of new shoes. You could smell it in the shop. When you got home and the shoes were delivered, you could smell it again. It was a real leather smell.

You got X-rayed and measured and fitted but you always had Band-Aids on your heels and round your toes for a few days.

You were always taking your shoes in for repair. Holes in the sole, a new heel, those lethal tin clips on the toes and heels. The repair shops were always small and dark. They sold second-hand suitcases as well.

The guy next door ran a shoe repair shop in his garage. He was furious when Dad bought his own last and repaired ours himself. Dad'd be out there at night, hammering and tapping away. The shoes often felt a bit uneven for a few days.

We were supposed to clean our shoes every day. Nugget or Kiwi polish. One brush for putting on the polish, one brush for polishing and then a miniature velvet cushion for buffing them up. Mum checked, then the teacher at school checked.

"You're not stepping out of this house without shoes." My mother insisted I wear shoes to school. She bought me silly looking leather sandals with toes. I used to get to the bottom of the street and hide them in a friend's garage. Everyone had bare feet. You were a real sissy for wearing shoes.

Our cousins came out from England and they thought we must be really poor because we never wore shoes. We knew they were Poms, because they did.

We had sandshoes, but not sneakers. You only wore sandshoes for sport. My grandmother used to say that only people like greyhound trainers wore sandshoes.

Plastic sandals were a real rage when they came in. They had moulded holes in the strap and they came in red and yellow as well as black and brown.

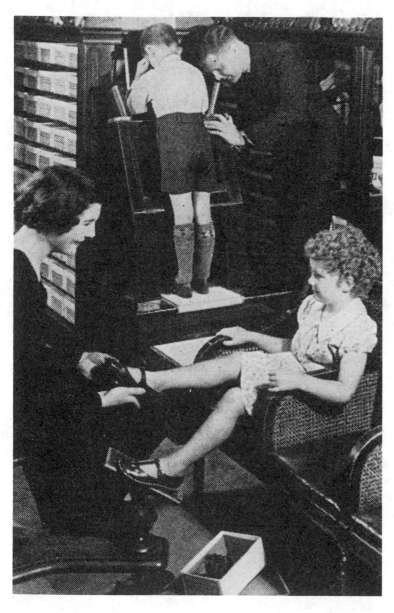

The right size was important.

146M1   146M2   146M3

146M4   146M5   146M6

Hats for every occasion.

Heads Means Hats

Hats were a standard part of Australian dress until almost the end of the 1960s. Men wore hats to work. Women wore hats out shopping. Children tried to avoid hats, but they were often unavoidable.

Mum bought me a deerstalker hat because I kept getting ear infections. It was bad enough with the flaps tied up on top, but I absolutely refused to wear them over my ears.

My mother knitted my hats and I hated them. What I wanted was a pretty little straw hat like the other girls wore to Sunday school.

You could tell what was going on by what the adults did with their hats. If Mum's friend came in and took off her hat, you knew she'd be staying. If a man came in and left his hat on, Mum would feel insulted. If Mum came in after shopping and flopped down with her hat still on, she'd had a terrible day, and watch out!

School Style

There had always been school uniforms, but in the 1950s these spread from private schools and the bigger public schools to even the smallest schools. They became a school status symbol, fitting in comfortably with the militaristic tendencies of schools.

I was terribly excited when our school got a uniform. We even had a sports uniform. Blue shorts and a white blouse. You had a yellow stripe on the shorts if you were in Yellow House and a red stripe if you were in Red.

Our school didn't have uniforms till I was in second class. I'd always envied my sister having a tunic. But once we got the uniform, we couldn't wear bare feet or even sandals in summer. There were a whole lot of rules about wearing your hat and blazer "in public", whatever that was.

If only we'd all been so neat!

The headmistress would start assembly in a really low tone, confiding how "a friend of the school" had rung her, to let her know that some girls had been seen on the train without their gloves. Sometimes, old girls of the school had rung up in tears because they'd seen girls without hats. Then we'd all sing the school song. They'd track down the gloveless girls and give them detentions. That was education.

When I was going off to boarding school, I got more clothes than I'd ever had in my life. It was all regulation school stuff, even down to navy blue underpants and singlets. Mum laid all the stuff out on her double bed. The only thing I liked was the red silk girdle on the gym tunic.

If our tunics were too short, the sewing teacher sewed brown paper round the hem. There was something dreadful about knees.

When you bought your uniform in a big department store in town, they sent the money upstairs in a pneumatic tube. The change would be sent back down the tube while they were wrapping your parcel.

When you reached a certain age, the Stamina suits came with a leather wallet in the pocket.

You got a set of project cards if you had a suit made of Crusader cloth.

They made hats part of the uniform, to make the school seem a bit more respectable. We refused to wear them. They couldn't cane 800 boys every day.

I loosened the knot in my tie and got a detention for "wearing a tie in an insolent manner".

Teen Fashion

Growing up was marked by the arrival of grown up clothes. Little boys got into long pants, girls began wearing stockings and lipstick. But it wasn't until the late 1950s that a 'teenage' market began to develop in clothes. Individuality was not encouraged. Cleanliness and neatness, paramount in childhood, remained important virtues, although not necessarily to the teenagers.

My first court shoes were pale brown with a brown and white bow. I still had to wear socks but I felt very superior to my little sister. Finally, it was high heels and stockings. I was thrilled, but I remember thinking I'd never be able to run down the hill again.

My first pair of long pants were so good. I'd been begging my mother to buy them for about ten years.

I felt humiliated wearing braces. I threw them away and told my mother that I wouldn't wear them any more. She asked me how I'd keep my trousers up. I hadn't thought about that.

I got a straight skirt when I was thirteen. I felt incredibly grown up. Unfortunately, I couldn't walk in it.

Beachwear for the Teenager

This is how their mothers would have liked them to look.

Winkle pickers were the thing. Long pointy shoes. You could have speared a cockroach.

Jeans were awful. Great wide things with turned up cuffs. They were a sort of country thing you wore with a checked shirt.

Stretch pants came in for girls. They were the first thing that made me look sexy.

We wore bermuda shorts and thought we were just it. Then there was the ultimate — stretch bermudas in purple and black check.

Getting a proper coat was a big thing — a topper coat or a car coat. You didn't take it off for about six months.

It's no wonder we wore fluorescent socks and lurex jackets. I was dressed in grey for the first fifteen years of my life.

CHAPTER SIX

Not the Dettol Mum

Miss Molly had a dolly who was sick, sick, sick.
She called for the doctor to come quick, quick, quick.
He wrote down on paper for a pill, pill, pill.
And said 'I'll be back in the morning for the bill, bill, bill.'

Miracles of Modern Medicine

The baby boomer was a child of science. Science, it was believed, had the answer to most problems. It held the key to progress and to the future. The atomic bomb had won the war, but the time had come to harness science to the betterment of mankind. Nowhere was this more evident than in medicine. Antibiotics cured many diseases and saved lives. As a result, far fewer children died. The parents of the baby boomers were a generation who had lost brothers and sisters in infancy. This left them with an anxiety about their own children's health, although happily, they could be fairly confident of rearing them to adulthood. They had faith in science, but not quite enough to entirely abandon their folk wisdom.

Childhood Ailments

The doctor, the representative of modern science, was the ultimate authority, but traditional remedies were not swept aside. Doctors gave injections and performed surgery, but mothers had bottles, potions and tonics with their own magical properties.

I was three when I got my first bee sting. My mother took out the sting and put on the blue bag she put in with the wash. I was amazed that it worked on washing *and* bee stings.

I had a fever and I had to soak in a tepid bath with Condy's Crystals. I did feel better, sitting there in the pale pink water.

I thought Mercurochrome was red so you could stop blood with blood. Having it all over your knees was a badge of honour.

They used Gentian Violet at school. You had purple knees for a week. It was never as good as Mercurochrome.

If you got bruises, you rubbed in a black paste called "Iodex". The wonderful thing was that it made them look more spectacular.

I went through childhood with permanently scabbed knees. I only stopped getting scabs when it all turned to solid scar tissue.

I was always trying to get my legs free of sores and scratches. Finally, they were right. My mother looked at my feet and told me I had tinea. She painted them with Friars Balsam and ruined my perfection.

Dettol on the gravel rash — it was torture.

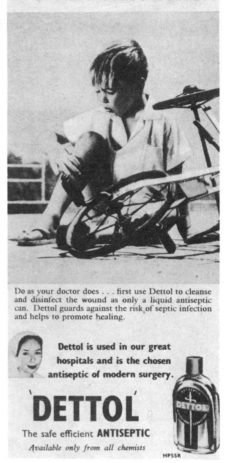

Mothers liked Dettol more than children.

Mumps, chickenpox, measles and colds were, as now, the standard childhood illnesses. Sometimes, these were spectacular in effect, sometimes disappointing.

I'd always wanted to get mumps and have my face swell up. I was terribly disappointed when I got them. Nothing happened to my face. I just felt sick.

When I had measles my mother shut me in a darkened room. I peeked through the blinds and Mum screeched in and said, "Don't do that. You'll go blind." I was terrified.

Chickenpox was so revolting. I felt really ashamed when I went back to school. I had scabs all over my face.

I loved staying home sick. My mother used to grate an apple and put sugar on it.

Mum made blancmange and custard when I was sick. She seemed to think I'd lost all my teeth.

"We'll build you up," Mum would say. That meant liver and brains and beef broth. I couldn't eat it. No wonder I was sick.

We used to get red hot flannels with eucalyptus oil put on our chests when we had colds. It felt good and it smelt lovely.

The moment we had a sniffle, Mum would get out the Vicks-Vapo rub. It was very comforting, lying in bed, getting your chest rubbed.

I used to sort through Mum's button collection when I was sick.

You'd sit over a basin of boiling water with Friars Balsam with a towel over your head and you'd inhale. The water was so hot that you were begging to come out.

I hated going back to school after a cold. Mum would pin a hanky on my pocket. It was revolting by the end of the day.

Thank God for tissues. We used to have old sheets, ripped into squares.

Socially Undesirable

Some diseases, although not inherently serious, resulted in social ostracism. Such diseases, while leading to a certain amount of discrimination, also had their own horrid fascination.

My friend had a wart on her index finger. The wart was always stained black with ink. She used to chew at it too. I didn't want to hold her hand in case I caught it.

A cure for a wart was for your friend to buy it. She'd give you some money and you were supposed to be cured. Of course, you had to be good friends.

You could cure a wart by tying a hair round it. The trick was keeping the hair on.

You could cure a stye by pressing a gold wedding ring against it. But no-one wanted to even touch you if you had a stye.

One kid was always getting boils. We wouldn't play with him.

When you got tinea, you used a matchstick to paint green stuff called Mycazol in between your toes. It stung like hell.

If you had nits in your hair, you always blamed the kid you thought you caught it from. The remedy for nits was purple paint on your head which lasted about two weeks longer than the nits.

It was bad enough wearing glasses, but I had to have a brown paper patch over one eye. My mother used to tell me that no-one cared about my eye. That wasn't true. One of the boys told me I couldn't play with them because I had a brown paper patch.

They had awful names for kids with glasses — "four eyes", "goggles", "cyclops". You learned to be tough.

I had to have an operation on my ears. My biggest fear wasn't the operation, but the thought of going to school with cottonwool in my ears.

IT'LL MAKE YOU BETTER

Agarol
A.P.C.s
Bex Powders
Bi-carb of soda
Blue Bags
Californian Syrup of Figs
Cascara
Condy's Crystals
Dettol
Eucalyptus oil
Friars Balsam
Gentian Violet
Indian Root Pills
Iodex
Irish Moss
Laxettes
Mercurochrome
Milk of Magnesia
Mycazol
Throaties
Ung-Vita
Vicks VapoRub
Vincents
Woods Great Peppermint Cure

Oh! To Have an Injury

If some diseases resulted in ostracism, broken bones carried a certain kudos. Similarly, stitches gave the injured child a certain glory. The more spectacular and bizarre the circumstances, the greater the glory.

I fell down a tree and neatly turned both my kneecaps inside out. I got them stitched up and was put to bed. I climbed out the window. I couldn't wait to show everybody.

My brother broke an arm and then a leg. He was encased in plaster. I thought if only such wonderful things happened to me.

I remember going to get my arm set. I looked at it and suddenly realised it was really crooked. I fainted.

What did one tonsil say to the other? You'd better get dressed. Doctor's taking us out tonight.

My mother told me my older sister had broken her leg. I was very disappointed when I saw her. I thought it would have broken right off.

I was always hurting myself. It drove my mother mad. I came in with a broken leg. She turned round and said, "For God's sake, why don't you walk properly?"

There was a girl at school who had fourteen stitches. Fourteen! No-one else could match that.

In Dire Peril

There were, of course, serious diseases. A scarlet fever epidemic closed down Victorian schools in the early 1950s. Mothers worried about reported outbreaks of diphtheria. Until the polio vaccine was introduced, polio was feared as a disease that could kill or cripple. In general, children took the threat more lightly than adults.

I had a friend whose sister had died in the polio epidemic in the early 1950s. After that, her parents bought her a grand piano. I used to look at my little sister and think about it. It seemed fair enough.

I had polio, but it wasn't serious. In fact, it was quite good fun. My mother was very worried and spoilt me rotten. Sometimes, after I'd got better, I used to wish I'd come out of it with one of those leg braces. I thought she would have kept on being nice.

A kid came back to school wearing leg braces and special boots. Nobody wanted to know. It looked too serious.

My little sister had diphtheria. Mum was hysterical, talking about her being "taken". I wondered who would take her and why, especially as she was so sick.

There was a diphtheria outbreak. Suddenly, every kid became an expert on the treatment. They cut your throat open, they tickled inside your throat with feathers, they blew things down through straws. It got more and more Dickensian. When the epidemic stopped, we stopped talking about it.

One of the most radical steps in reducing child mortality was the introduction of the polio vaccine in 1956. Mass immunisations were done through schools. Children were less enthusiastic about the idea than adults.

There was this kid who was frightened of needles. When the polio sister came round, we egged this kid on. We told her how big the needle was and how much it hurt. It backfired because she became completely hysterical. Her mother came down to the school to calm her down. She didn't have much success. The rest of us started to feel very nervous.

Everyone made a big joke about polio shots, just like we made jokes about polio. When it came to the point, we were terrified.

Just Checking

The various education departments also introduced dental checks and regular health checks. Like school milk, they may have improved the health of the nation, but children saw them as an imposition.

I hated, I just hated the sister coming because she'd call out your weight. I was a fat kid and the other kids would yell "Fatso, Fatso". I can't tell you what torment it was. I still hate having a medical checkup because of that.

I hated getting my eyes tested. The sister was really patronising. "Is the lion in his cage or out of his cage? Has the doggy got the light on his nose?" I refused to answer and she got quite snappy and told me I'd have to have glasses unless I behaved myself. I had to have glasses anyway.

It was humiliating getting sick at school. When a kid vomited in the playground, someone else had to throw a bucket of sand over it.

The sick bay always had a really uncomfortable stretcher with a prickly grey blanket. It smelt of disinfectant and had that really thick lino on the floor.

Have your eyes been checked lately? No, they've always been plain blue.

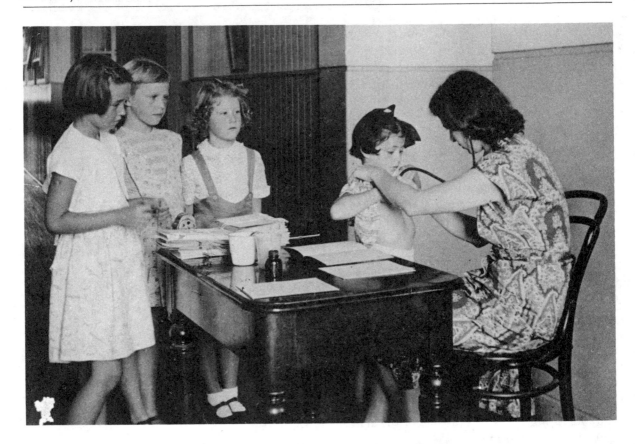

Check ups were a public occasion.

I was waiting outside the caravan where they set up the mobile dental service. Some kids had already been in. The nurse came out with an enamel bowl of bloody water and tipped it out next to us.

Teeth Terrors

Before the introduction of fluoride into the water supply, holes in teeth were almost unavoidable. Unfortunately, dentists' equipment was far more primitive than today's high tech machinery. No sleight of hand could disguise the fact that an assault of major proportions was taking place in the mouth.

I remember the foot-powered drills. You'd have this excruciating, throbbing pain in your mouth and you could see his foot pumping away, in time to it.

The noise was awful. It was like a piece of stonemason's equipment going full bore.

I had to get a filling done when I was on holiday up the country. The dentist had his chair in the front room of his house. He was old and he had the shakes badly. He came towards me, with the drill vibrating slowly in his shaky old hands. He probably drilled the wrong tooth. I was in shock for a week afterwards anyway.

I always went to the dentist on a school day, so I got the rest of the afternoon off. My mouth would be numb, but I'd always have a strawberry milkshake at Joe's on the way home. One afternoon, I lost control of my entire face and the milkshake started spurting back out of one side of my mouth. It caused a fountain effect over which I was powerless. Joe looked at me, sitting there in my school suit and cap. From the look on his face, he obviously classified me as a typical private school prick.

We always used Ipana tooth powder. I remember the wonderful day when we got a tube of banana flavoured toothpaste.

I couldn't work out how they got the stripe in Stripe toothpaste. It was the miracle of modern science.

Hospital Horrors

If dentists were traumatic, hospitals were even more so. On the principle of 'what you don't know won't hurt you', parents whisked children into hospital with no prior preparation. Getting your tonsils, adenoids and appendix out was far more common than it is today, and was considered by some parents to be an almost necessary cleansing process. In hospital, there was little consideration of children's emotional needs. Parents were discouraged from protracted visits on the grounds that these would upset their children. The system was hard on all concerned.

Mum got me dressed in my new pyjamas, new dressing gown and new slippers. I knew something was up. I started screaming as they took me out to the car.

I had quite a few operations. I'd be wheeled in and they'd pull down the mask for the anaesthetic. I always thought it was a telephone and I always wanted to ask why. But I was out before I could.

The only good part of hospital was taking your tonsils home in a bottle.

We had half hour visits. I used to scream and scream for my mother not to go. It embarrassed her that I was such a sook.

I wanted to go to hospital and get something out. I never had my appendix out, or my adenoids or my tonsils. I had no scars or stitches. I never even had a filling. It seemed desperately unfair.

Adult Ailments

There were many conditions and illnesses only adults had, but which were, nevertheless, fascinating to children.

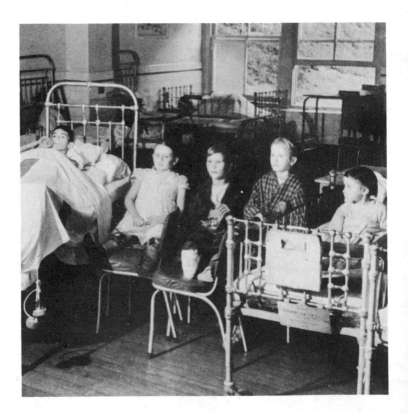

Being in hospital wasn't easy but at least there were other children.

These were often unmentionable, a fact that made them even more mysterious and interesting.

My mother warned me that unless I brushed my teeth, they'd all fall out. I couldn't see the problem. I thought false teeth would be wonderful.

My father used to rub this yellow cream into his head every night. He explained it was to stop him going bald. Within a year, he was completely bald. He stopped using the cream.

Our grandfather used to wear a surgical corset under his longjohns. It was the most interesting thing about him. We tried to get a good look at it to work out what it was for. We wouldn't have dreamt of asking.

We used to hear mutters about haemorrhoids and piles. I knew they were very private. I read all the advertisements and knew all the remedies, but had no idea what these strange adult diseases actually were.

But It's Good for You!

Children were also subjected to various medications and tonics, the exact purpose of which was not always clear. These were often force-fed and usually unwelcome.

My mother used to dose us with something called Cascara. I had no idea what it was for, but I hated it.

We used to have a spoonful of Agarol. "It'll make you feel better," Mum would say. It was useless telling her you felt fine.

I was very taken with chocolate flavoured Laxettes. So taken with them that I had a whole bottle. I've never been able to eat Laxettes or chocolate since then.

I loved the Throaties ad. "If you've got a tickle or a cough, laugh it off, with Throaties!"

There was the Irish Moss Syrup — "Sip, Sip, Sip," they said on the wireless, as if it was a fantastic drink.

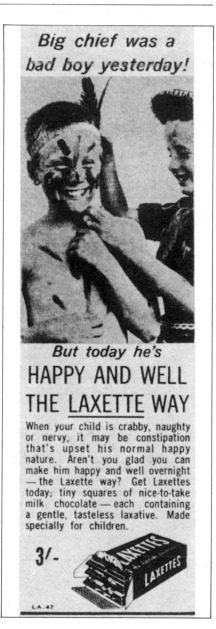

We used to have Indian Root Pills. Dad used to say it didn't matter what they were made of. The important thing was that they did you good. I always had the idea they had snake's eggs in them.

There was Woods Great Peppermint Cure, with rhymes up in all the trams. It tasted amazingly powerful, but I don't know that it actually did anything.

We were regularly dosed with cod-liver oil and all sorts of other medicines. It's amazing what the human bowel can withstand.

I felt sick all through my childhood. It was probably all the cures we had.

We had Californian Syrup of Figs which was just horrible. Fortunately, it was on a fairly irregular basis. Mother would suddenly decide we were all "sickly" and dose us up for a week. Then she'd forget about it, thank God.

My mother felt quite superior because she was into Ung-Vita which was a vitamin tonic. All the other mothers were into laxatives. Thank God for science.

Milk of Magnesia was an important ingredient of my childhood. Without it, my mother told us, you couldn't grow properly.

We were dosed for worms every second week. My mother thought we had worms because we were all so skinny. The medicine made you nauseous for days. It was no wonder we were skinny.

CHAPTER SEVEN

Myths and Misconceptions

My mother said, I never should,
Play with the gypsies, in the wood,
If I did, she would say,
Naughty girl to disoday.'

True or False?

Every childhood has had its mythology — its particular bogeymen under the bed, its man in the moon to grant wishes, its hidden treasure, its fairies at the bottom of the garden. Amongst children, myths are not discussed, but simply accepted. Some myths are local, but many of these are variations on a theme. For instance, almost every suburb has a wicked witch in some form.

Some myths continue for generations, others stop after a few years. For instance, the saving of silver paper was killed stone-dead by the introduction of tinfoil as a cooking aid. The allegedly poisonous ice scrapings from the inside of the freezer compartment died with the invention of frost-free refrigeration. With the introduction of the sabin vaccine, polio myths have ceased to become part of childhood. In every generation, many of the children's myths have to do with health, or with the dangers of the environment.

My mother told me that if I sucked the end of magpie feathers, I'd get polio. I asked another kid if it was true and he said it was. I was really scared because I had sucked so many magpie feathers. It felt like the polio was inside and one day I'd wake up in an iron lung.

We weren't allowed to eat desiccated coconut because it was a source of polio germs. It came from a country where polio was rife.

Step on a crack,
You'll marry a black.
Step on a hair,
You'll marry a bear.

Needless to say there was no truth to this scurrilous rumour!

We were strictly brought up not to drink out of bubblers. Dogs drank out of them. The theory was you could get worms. One of my strongest childhood memories was of seeing a wire haired fox terrier standing on its hind legs licking a bubbler. I knew Mum hadn't lied.

We all believed that licorice was made out of ox blood. One boy had been to a licorice factory where he saw oxen being led in one end and licorice extruding out the other end. It never stopped us eating it.

It was rumoured that every Ford Slimming Tablet contained a tapeworm egg. The tapeworm hatched inside you and ate your excess weight. I was horrified when I saw my mother taking one. She told me she'd never heard such nonsense in her life.

Living in the inner city, we were never in any danger of being bitten by a goanna. It still seemed important that we know that a goanna bite never heals.

We loved scraping the ice out of the fridge, despite the warnings of my mother that it contained deadly poisonous aluminium. That didn't worry us much because Mum also used to complain about her custard going grey from the aluminium saucepans. It was when a kid told us that the ice had electricity in it, that it became really dangerous.

The story was that if you made faces and the wind changed you'd stay that way. We knew it was crap, but you could sometimes use it on little kids.

The hydatid tapeworm lurked everywhere according to my mother — from dog poo to underdone pork.

If you swallowed chewing gum, it stuck the sides of your stomach together. That meant major surgery. I didn't mention it to my mother when I happened to swallow a piece.

If you swallowed an apricot pip, the apricot tree would grow out of your mouth. The thought of having to prune it back to your tonsils was a great deterrent.

The Wicked Old Witch

Many of the myths of childhood had to do with dangerous people. Often, these were told by adults, to curb the adventurous spirit of children. Once they took root in the children's imagination, they developed a life of their own.

Gypsies not only kidnapped little kids. They could also take your mother's purse out of her very hand by looking deep into her eyes. You could tell a gypsy immediately by the gold earrings and the spotted scarf. In the 1950s no-one dressed like that, probably not even gypsies.

I moved around a lot as a kid, but every town or suburb had a wicked woman or a wicked old witch. It was best if she lived in a tumbledown old house with an overgrown garden. In some cases, she was a perfectly ordinary old lady living in red brick suburbia.

Cross my heart and hope to die,
If I ever tell a lie.

We used to persecute the old witch, throwing stones on the roof or ringing the doorbell. She never complained to our parents. To us, that proved conclusively she was a witch.

I was too scared to walk past her house. I remember walking the long way round, then one day, getting the courage to go past, running. My heart was beating so fast.

If you looked at VWs which were going 33 miles per hour, you could see a swastika on the hub-cap. It was the Nazis' way of getting back at us for being beaten in the war. The trick was to find a VW doing 33 miles per hour.

Easy Pickings

Many myths had to do with the possibilities of making big money. The actual amount of money was discussed at length. In spite of the lure of wealth, the plans were rarely put into action.

A Black Prince cicada was worth anywhere between ten bob and ten quid. There were the sceptics who said you'd only get two and six. The story was that the chemist boiled them down to make some very rare and precious medicine.

It wasn't the Black Prince itself that was worth so much, but the ruby on its forehead. That was the trick — to get one with a good ruby.

I took the first Black Prince cicada I ever found into the chemist. I'd been told on reliable authority that the going rate was five quid and I'd spent it down to the last penny. But the chemist just looked at me and said, "Not today sonny." Then he went back to work. I couldn't believe it.

Even more rare than the Black Prince was the Union Jack cicada. It was striped red, white and blue. My mate and I were up and down trees, going berserk searching for these creatures. We were always convinced we'd just missed one.

My brothers found a Wrigleys wrapper with the full alphabet on it. We thought we were made for life. We sent it in with a letter and waited and waited for the money to come back.

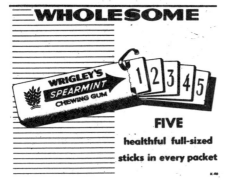

If only these were Black Princes!

We'd get a chewing gum wrapper where the letters went up to "w" or "y" and try and forge the rest. I used to think I'd done quite well. I'd show it to my sister and she'd tell me it was hopeless. It was worth going to some trouble because it was worth ten thousand pounds.

You could get silver paper from chocolate wrappers and cigarette paper. With the cigarette paper you had to peel off the layer of tissue. But it was very good quality. Milk bottle tops

Can you keep a secret?
I don't believe you can.
Don't laugh, don't cry.
Do the best you can.

were awful because you had to wash them. Even then they wouldn't stick to the ball properly. You were supposed to send the silver ball off when it was about as big as a basketball.

We made a silver ball at school. We brought milk bottle tops from home and also used the ones on the school milk. Someone had the job of washing them. There was a vague idea we would send it to the Queen, but the teacher wasn't very specific.

I'd been told you sent the silver balls in to help make aeroplanes. It was selfish to make one just for yourself.

Silver balls were for starving people in India. How they used them, I have no idea.

My sister and I made an enormous silver ball. We were really proud of it, but when we finished, no-one could tell us where to send it.

Chain letters seemed like a terrific way of making money. I never believed my parents when they told me it was a fraud. I thought they were against me getting rich.

I sent off all my pocket money in a chain letter. When I didn't get the thousand pounds, I was furious. I wanted Dad to do something, but he wouldn't.

Tall Tales

Some myths of childhood were simply warnings against unforeseen dangers, or casual explanations of the way things were. Some were manufactured by older children or parents. Children believed them and developed them further.

My sister used to tell me that fairies had to change their wings. She said they left the old ones under the mushrooms near the chook shed. I'd go down there and actually see them. It wasn't until years later that I found out she pulled the wings off cicadas and left them there. It spoilt the idea of fairies forever.

I believed that if you spat on your hands first, it didn't hurt so much when you got the cane. The teacher must have believed it too, because he stopped boys doing it.

My mother hated cooking sausages. She told us they were made out of the sawdust on the butcher's floor and what he scraped off the walls, all stuffed into pig's guts. We believed her, but we still loved sausages.

We believed that Sao biscuits were manufactured in a special way so it was impossible to eat three dry Saos in a minute. We used to have contests. It was impossible.

Unravelling a golf ball was terrific fun, because we knew the ball in the centre was deadly poison. As you got down to the centre, you had to be really careful not to touch it.

My brother used to chase me with the bag from the inside of a golf ball, threatening to squirt it at me. I was convinced I'd die.

One for a kiss, two for a wish,
Three for a letter, four for two
*   better.*
Five for silver, six for gold,
Seven for a secret never told.

Misunderstandings

Lack of communication between children and teachers, combined with rote learning, lead to misconceptions, which were often remarkably persistent.

We had a hymn about "Gladly, the cross I'd bear for Jesus". I sang it for years, wondering about the connection between Jesus and the cross-eyed bear.

I used to sing "Hark the Herald Angels Sing", with an absolute conviction that the Herald referred to was *The Sydney Morning Herald*. I thought the Herald angels were like the David Jones choir.

At assembly, we had a recitation to "cheerfully obey my parents, my teachers and the law. Amen. Hands down". I never realised that the hands down was to do with taking your hand off your heart. I thought it was an additional Amen.

My mother carefully explained to me what the horizon was. For years, I was convinced it was the spot on the top of the big hill at Gerringong.

CHAPTER EIGHT

The Devil and the Deep Blue Sea

Hear the pennies dropping,
Listen how they fall,
Every one for Jesus,
He shall have them all.

God on Our Side

In the post-war era, most people went to church. Many families went every week and the vast majority of people went at least several times a year. Parents felt obliged to give their children some religious training, even if they were not ardent believers or churchgoers themselves. Religious differences were, for the most part, divisions amongst Christian sects. But despite the heavy hand of orthodoxy, children had their own views.

I found out about hell and went into immediate terror. It wasn't the next life I was worried about. I thought I'd fall into a gutter and be swept down into the furnaces.

I came from a strict Methodist family who spent all of Sunday at church. I never entertained the possibility that God actually existed.

My friend told me about the soul. It was a white strip across your forehead, just in front of the brain. For every bad thing you did, a black spot appeared on it. I had an instant vision of my own, very nastily spotted and grubby.

I got God horribly mixed up with fairy stories. I thought heaven was full of unicorns and extinct animals.

My father told me I could pray for whatever I wanted and God would answer it in his own way. That was the escape clause.

I really liked the idea of God. My parents and teachers might be against me, but I had God on my side.

Sunday School

For most children, Sunday school was the beginning of formal religious education. Most parents insisted on attendance for over a couple of years, but success in inculcating religious belief was variable.

I was terribly religious for a few years. I loved going to Sunday school because I was allowed to wear my best dress. That was the main reason.

You got a stamp to paste in your book every time you went. If you got a full book at the end of the year, you got a book of Bible stories. What they didn't take into account was that one book of Bible stories was enough for anyone.

I saw all the kids going off to the Sunday school picnic. I told my mother I wanted to go. She explained you had to go to Sunday school for a year. The next year I went, every single Sunday. At the end of the year I went to the Sunday school picnic. I never went to Sunday school again.

You had to go to Mass, because the nuns would be onto you at school on Monday unless you did.

We had a Sunday school money box in the shape of a black boy. You put money in his hands.

The Sunday school teacher always had a great bundle of rolled up pictures. She'd get one or two out and hang them up. They were very distinctive. All the people had very vague expressions on their faces. They all wore togas in washed out colours. There were always a few palm trees and sometimes a stone archway in the background.

We were always giving money to starving blacks in Africa. I used to get confused because we were shown pictures of happy, laughing African children. It wasn't until the Freedom from Hunger Campaign that we saw what our money was actually for.

Matthew, Mark, Luke and John.
Next door neighbour,
Pass it on.

Getting certificates was a sign of spiritual progress.

Praise the Lord

Church was also obligatory for many children. It was a test not only of religious fervour, but of the ability to sit still and pretend to know what to do.

I went to church in total confusion. I never knew when to kneel, how to find the hymns or whether I was supposed to pray out loud with the minister or silently. I was a religious write-off.

The first time I went to church my grandfather told me to copy everything he did. The first thing he did was take off his hat. I took mine off and some lady jammed it back on my head. "Girls leave their hats on," she hissed.

I had a burst of religious fervour and volunteered to be an altar boy. I'd lost the religious fervour a few weeks later, but I had to serve out my time.

I loved the choir and the hymns. I'd get a very religious feeling. The sermon really spoilt it.

The Other Half

Religious tolerance in Australia meant putting up with other people who had the same basic beliefs. In the post-war era, almost everyone was nominally Christian, except for a small population of Jews and a few atheists. There were no exotic sects such as the Hare Krishnas, nor were there Muslims or Hindus. The major religious divisions were between Catholics and Protestants, with some minor reverberations between the Protestant sects.

We used to fight the Catholic boys, because they were Catholics. But it was sporadic. The rest of the time we got on with them okay.

There were definite divisions between Catholics and Protestants. Catholics had Vitabrits, Protestants had Weet-Bix, Catholics took Disprin, Protestants took Asprin, Catholics drank Tiny Tips, Protestants drank Liptons, Catholics used Vegemite, Protestants used Marmite. It didn't affect children much except we Catholic children played with Montini, which was better quality than Lego.

I asked our Parish priest what Anglicans believed in. He looked down at me and said, "Nothing much son. Nothing much."

My mother wanted to be liberal with her children and she told us we could be whatever religion we wanted. I said I wanted to be Catholic. I quickly realised the choice was Presbyterian or Presbyterian.

I wanted to send off for one of those booklets explaining Catholicism, but I knew my mother wouldn't approve.

My Dad said there was nothing wrong with Catholics except they wanted to put Australia in the hands of a foreign power and get rid of the Queen.

Protestants were the Antichrist and we weren't allowed to play with them.

Here's the church,
Here's the steeple.
Open the door,
And see all the people.

Catholic dogs,
Jump like frogs,
In and out of water.

Catholics, Catholics,
Ring the bell.
All the Proddies
Go to hell.

We Baptists weren't allowed to have pre-marital sex because it could lead to dancing.

We heard that Masons "rode the goat". The Catholic kids hung round the Masonic Hall, but we never even saw a goat. We still believed it though.

Scripture Once a Week

If children did not get their religious education through Sunday school or church, they still got a hearty dose of scripture at school. Visiting ministers were regular in their attendance at schools and made every attempt to make up for deficiencies in religious education elsewhere.

The first scripture lesson I recall was on the crucifixion. It was fire and brimstone. By the end of the lesson, I felt as if my hands were nailed to the desk.

The minister used the scripture lesson to castigate children who didn't come to Sunday school or whose parents didn't go to church. You had to sit in the front so you got the word of God, and then promise to go next Sunday.

Let us pray together for eternal salvation.

The Presbyterian Moderator visited the school once a year. He wore a sort of Pilgrim costume, with black stockings and gaiters. It was understood we'd be given a day off if we didn't laugh at his clothes.

Catholic scripture in a public school was awful. There weren't many of us. They used to upbraid us because our parents weren't making the sacrifice to send us to Catholic schools. We went back to class feeling as if we were in the grip of the Protestant devils.

In the convent, everything was religious. All the things you wrote at the top of your books, the stickers teachers gave out if you were good, then religious education on top of that.

I got to high school and explained to the deputy headmaster that I wouldn't be going to scripture because I was a non-believer. He just looked at me. "There are no atheists in my school sonny."

All I learnt in scripture lessons was to recite the names of the books of the Bible ... Genesis, Exodus, Leviticus, etc. I was acclaimed as a model student, but I can't remember ever actually having read the Bible.

Religious Rituals

Neither the Catholic nor Protestant churches in Australia were particular ritualistic. However, some rituals did play an important part in the lives of children.

I used to worry about my sister not being christened until she was a year old. I was convinced if she died, she'd go to Hell. My mother never saw the urgency.

I missed out on being christened. I used to whinge about it to Mum. She told me it was only for babies.

First communion was like getting your first filling. Scary, but you could say you'd done it.

I really felt holy when I had my first communion. I spoilt it when I came out of the church and threw up.

Salvation Army free from sin. Went to heaven in a kerosene tin.

First communion was a serious business.

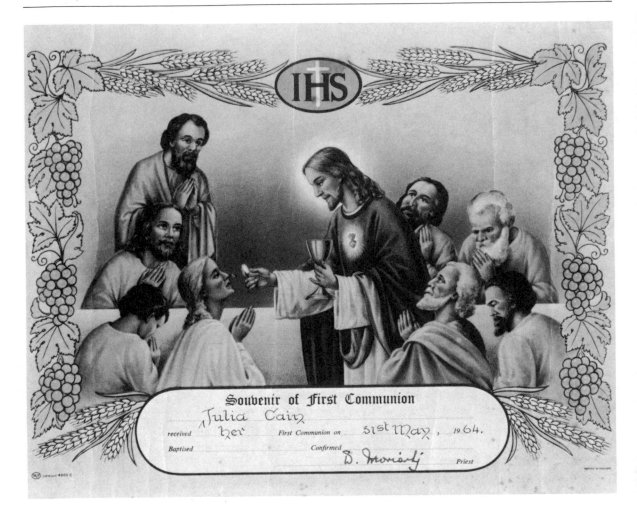

Souvenir of First Communion

Julia Cain

received her First Communion on 31st May, 1964.

Baptised _____ Confirmed _____

D. Moriarty   Priest

But afterwards there was another certificate.

The main thing about being confirmed was going to the confirmation classes. You organised it so you got confirmed at the same time as the boy you liked.

I was disappointed when I was confirmed. I felt exactly the same.

Friends at Fellowship

Fellowship was an attempt to get adolescents to stay with their church against the competing claims of less respectable social activities. Sometimes the strategy worked, sometimes for the wrong reasons.

We used to go to the Presbyterian fellowship because they had the prettiest girls.

I was quite devout, but I far preferred church. There were those dreary fellowship socials, everyone too shy to talk. Supper was jam sponge and soggy Jatz biscuits.

They used the fellowship to conscript Sunday school teachers. I didn't want anything more to do with Sunday school, so I stopped going.

The big high of my years at fellowship was the Billy Graham crusade. We all went together in a bus and we all went forward for Jesus. It was very emotional. After that, church and fellowship seemed to lack something.

I went to fellowship and became a Sunday school teacher, then a monitor. I thought everyone did it.

When God first made the world,
He made man the strongest,
But just to give the girls a
*   chance,*
He made their fingers longest.

Rays of sunshine,
Falls of rain,
Make the earth,
Smile again.
A happy smile,
A kindly thought,
Help us live,
The life we ought.

CHAPTER NINE

Crime and Punishment

Tell tale tit,
Your tongue will split,
And all the little puppy dogs
Will have a little bit.

Wait Till your Father gets Home

Modern psychology had made little impression on the average Australian parent of the post-war era. At that time, there was more discussion about the physical health of children than about their mental health. To many parents, it was clear that if children did the wrong thing, they should be punished, often physically. Threats of punishment and of temporary or permanent abandonment, played a part in keeping children in line.

My mother would get sick of me and threaten to give me to the garbage collectors. At the time, I thought she was perfectly serious. I developed a strong dislike of garbage collectors.

My mother used to threaten to send me to a boys home. I was frightened when I was small, but it ceased to work when I actually got interested in going.

The worst threat was "Wait till your father gets home".

My younger brother was furious because he got spanked and I didn't. One day I'd done something terrible and my little brother insisted I get spanked for it. Dad took me into the bedroom and said, "You scream while I hit the bed." I felt a bit guilty.

Tinker, tailor,
Soldier, sailor,
Rich man,
Poor man,
Beggarman,
Thief!

Dad used to lock us in the shed if we played up. I kept a few books under the bench. He'd come down and say, "Are you sorry now?" Once, when I was half way through a chapter, I said "No, I'm not." I stayed in there till I finished the whole book that time.

School Discipline

Today, the cane isn't used in most public schools. Twenty years ago, it was commonly used. It was regarded with far more fear than other standard punishments of being kept in, writing lines or picking up papers. Classrooms were more rigidly organised and transgressions were more common.

The worst thing was being sent to the headmaster. Our class was in a portable classroom at the bottom of the school and you had to walk all the way up to the office with this note from the teacher. It said what you'd done and how many cuts of the cane you were to get.

I was being kept in one day and I desperately wanted to play with the other kids down the bush. The teacher went out for a minute and I climbed out the window. I couldn't believe I'd done it. The most amazing thing was that the teacher never mentioned it.

Shoplifting and Stealing

'Thou shalt not steal' was a maxim that was strongly impressed on the young. In the long run, it was generally effective. In the short term, few children were entirely resistant to temptation.

I stole a pound note out of my mother's purse. That was a lot of money for a child and I wanted to get rid of it as quickly as I could. I went to the corner store and asked for a pound of bananas. I thought it would take care of the pound, so I was horrified when I got silver and a ten bob note in change. It felt as if the crime was snowballing. I had no idea how to get rid of the money.

There was a little girl and she had a little curl,
Right in the middle of her forehead.
When she was good, she was very very good,
And when she was bad, she was horrid.

Mum used to keep her money on top of the wardrobe. She didn't trust banks. I climbed up and got about forty quid — an enormous amount. Me and my mates buried it in Andy Gordon's backyard. I knew I was done for when I saw Andy Gordon coming past the kitchen window one Saturday lunch. It was the expression on his face. I started crying before he even got to the back door.

WHAT WE CALLED THE LOOT

Tray — threepence
Zac — sixpence
Deena or a bob — a shilling
Quid — a pound
Spin or a fiver — five pounds
Brick or a tenner — ten pounds

Shoplifting was more of a challenge than stealing from parents. Skill and daring, rather than the spoils them-selves were the attraction.

I promised Ross Andrews that I'd teach him to steal from Woolies. In exchange, he promised not to tell on me for the things I'd already pinched.

I stole some cheap rings from Woolies. When my mother found out, she hit the roof. She told me how humiliated she'd feel when she took them back and explained to the manager. I found the rings a couple of months later in her drawer. I was disillusioned.

I remember walking out of Coles with two little plastic dolls in my pocket. I never felt so scared in my life. I could see the prison walls.

CHILDHOOD CIGARETTE MEMORIES

Lucky Strike
Ardath
Craven A
Capstan
Peter Jackson
Three 3
Chesterfield
Du Maurier
Viscount

Smoking and Drinking

Neither adults nor children regarded cigarettes as a serious health hazard. Children were warned that smoking would stunt their growth, but against the immediate sophistication they offered, this did not weigh heavily. The attraction *and* the difficulty with cigarettes was that they were forbidden to children and had to be obtained by stealth. The same conditions applied to alcohol.

Our first cigarettes were dried grass rolled in dunny paper.

I stole a whole packet of Ardath from my Dad. I went down the creek with my mate. We each smoked one and went bright green. We decided to come back another day to finish them off. I was really relieved when they got wet.

I'd steal my mother's Craven A's and smoke them in the outside dunny.

My father said to me when I was fourteen, "I can't stop you smoking, but you're not to pinch mine." I don't know how he knew.

Four kids and one cigarette and we thought we were impressing the girls.

I used to think American cigarettes were better. There was one called "Spud", a menthol. It was like a very bad general anaesthetic.

Mum caught me sneaking a cup of sherry when I was ten. "You'll end up like your grandmother," she said. That scared me.

We decided it would prove we were grown up if we drank a glass of gin. Somebody must have been watering it down, because it didn't have much effect at all.

Some of the brands we started off on.

We stole a bottle of beer, but we had nothing to open it with.

Buy Now, Pay Later

Mail-order crime was usually the result of impulse buying, rather than of premeditated theft. There was an unpleasant moment when the realisation struck that funds were not available. The trouble was, they *knew* your address.

I'm the king of the castle
And you're the dirty rascal.

I ordered a set of Seven Seas stamps in the name of Jason Paris. I didn't have the money, so I had to write as Howard Paris and tell them that my brother Jason had sadly passed away. I explained that unfortunately, he had disposed of the stamps before his death. I got caught up in it and I put a big sign on my wall, "RIP, Jason Paris".

I ordered a set of embroidered hankies on approval for my mother's birthday. They were really expensive and not very nice, but I didn't even have the postage to send them back. The letters were getting really nasty. I even thought about stealing the hankies back from my mother, but that seemed really low.

I remember the demand for payment on some stamps. I felt sick. It was like receiving a death notice during the war. I was too scared to tell my parents.

Mind your Language!

The children of the 1950s and 1960s usually led lives that were far more sheltered than children of today. Adults may have sworn, but for children, bad language was forbidden.

Jinks, jeeze and blasted was as far as you got. Otherwise, you'd get a smack over the head.

My father used to come home drunk and talk about bloody this and bloody that. My mother would send us to bed.

I saw "fuck" written on the pavement and I asked my mother what it meant. She said it was a word used by people who didn't know how to express themselves properly and I must never, ever say it.

Was Wagging Wonderful?

Wagging school was a serious offence, but one for which surprisingly few children were caught.

I convinced my friend we should wag school just for the afternoon. I told her I knew how to do a note in running writing. It was easy. Running writing was just scribble. When it came to the point, it didn't really look all that convincing.

We went up to Bondi headland, but we had to keep hidden in case any of our mothers were around. We ate all our lunches at about 10 o'clock. Then we had to sit there in the cold till school came out and we could go home.

I used to go and sit in the newsreel theatre when I wagged school. You'd always be a bit worried in case the manager noticed you were in uniform and reported you.

I used to write my own notes for wagging school. My mother wrote one when I was sick and they were convinced it was a forgery.

I threatened to run away from home. "Go," said my mother.

Don't Play With Matches!

Fire and fireworks presented particularly attractive opportunities for children. Probably due to their own experiences as children, modern day bureaucrats have banned the use of fire crackers by children.

Tuppeny bungers were just amazing. You could blow up letterboxes or shove them down a pipe with marbles and fire them. They were lethal if they came out the wrong way.

I set the whole backyard alight and I thought my father would give me a terrible thrashing. The flames seemed terribly high, but Dad was standing there calmly hosing them. I couldn't understand it. He and the man next door were just laughing.

We used a whole lot of tuppeny bungers to blow up a Portaloo. It was the ultimate joke.

When the space race started, we began designing our own rockets. Once, we decided to send ants into space in a soft drink bottle. It was lucky we weren't killed.

One cracker night my brother was teasing us, threatening to light his rocket inside, putting the match near it. Suddenly it

HOT MEMORIES

Tom thumbs
Tuppeny bungers
Sparklers
Catherine wheels
Roman candles
Mount Vesuviuses
Rockets
Jumping jacks
Cones

The gang at cracker night.

went woosh, along the hall. The house was filled with red smoke and there, was a black rocket trail along the wall.

One year, the richest kid in the neighbourhood brought all his crackers in a leather suitcase. He was going to save them till last. Then there was this enormous bang. The suitcase went about 6 feet into the air. There were rockets driving into the ground and catherine wheels spinning out of control, bungers going off like gunfire. For a moment, the suitcase was silhouetted against the bonfire and then disintegrated in midair.

Just Enjoying Ourselves

Neighbourhood fights were a feature of suburban and town life. They may not have been serious, but were often painful.

We always had a fight in the choko season. They hurt and if they were smashed open, they left an awful sticky juice on your skin.

My mother secretly approved of choko fights because it meant she didn't have to make choko jam or choko preserve.

Acorns could hit hard if you were a good shot. They were lethal with a slingshot.

All the boys were warned by the headmaster about throwing stones. But there was one corner on the way home where they'd hide. The stones would come out low and hit you on the legs.

I wasn't allowed to have chewing gum. I got into a chewing gum fight. It was all through my hair, on my clothes and stuck on my face. I told my mother it wasn't my fault.

Finders keepers,
Losers weepers.

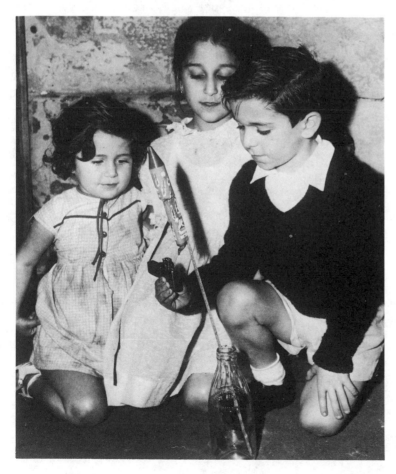

An explosive experience.

Liar, liar, pants on fire.
Nose is longer than a telephone
  wire.

I pushed a kid down the waterfall — just because he had red hair. I felt okay about it when I knew he wasn't dead.

If you hated somebody in the neighbourhood, you'd wait till dark and then throw gravel on the roof. It was only effective on a tin roof.

There were even more subtle forms of assault, refined over the years and passed down through generations of children.

You'd get a spit ball on your ruler and flick it towards the board when the teacher had his back turned.

The old post office nibs were a great missile.

We had an old nun at school who'd doze off during lessons. One day I crept up and tied her shoe laces together. She was fully conscious when she was belting me.

We'd ring up someone we didn't like from the public phone box and shout "bugger". Trouble was, you had to shout so loud you usually copped it from one of the neighbours.

We'd run up and knock on doors and then run away. After a couple of times, you began to look for more sophisticated things to do.

The parcel with a piece of string was good in theory. You'd yank it away when they went to pick it up, but it never worked out in practice. The string got caught or someone giggled.

You wrapped a piece of dog poo in paper and then set it alight on the front door step, rang the bell and ran away. Your enemy was supposed to come out, stamp out the fire and get dog poo all over their shoes. To tell you the truth, we never got organised with the dog poo.

CHAPTER TEN

Train Sets and Bride Dolls

My mother told me,
She would buy me,
a rubber dolly.
But when I told her
I kissed a soldier
She would not buy me
a D.. O.. L.. L.. Y.
(skipping rhyme)

·Made to Last

In the post-war era, toys were a twice yearly event — given on your birthday and at Christmas. Other than that, unless a grandmother got soft-hearted or soft-headed, the baby boomer relied on the walking horses or cowboy figures at the bottom of the corn flakes packet. This comparative paucity of toys wasn't due to stinginess and lack of generosity of parents. It was simply the way people lived. Toys were not the throwaway items they so often are today. Toys were made to be used until they wore out.

The very first toys I remember were unpainted wooden blocks. They had belonged to my cousin and someone else before her. They were incredibly smooth. As well as the square ones and the rectangles, there were arches and slides and parapets. You could knock up a pretty good castle.

We had a set of soldiers that had been in the family for ever. Some had buggered up arms and the rest wouldn't stand up straight. You weren't allowed to let the baby suck them because they were made of lead.

Toys, especially those for small children, didn't actually do anything. Remote control was not only unheard of, but not even thought of. It was either pull along or push along. However, there was some action, especially for boys, in the form of guns.

I got a Roy Rogers gun when I was seven. I was convinced the handle was real silver, even when it began to chip. But the best thing was that it was a cap gun, with the big size caps. They made a terrific bang and actually smoked. I remember, holding it in front of me, just watching it smoke.

The caps were always getting stuck and you'd have to adjust the roll to get it going again. Always in the middle of a shoot-out.

'When Johnny comes marching home.'

I lost my cap gun the day I shot my mother in the head to wake her up. She'd had enough.

Toys for Girls and Toys for Boys

Girls had to be content with more pedestrian pursuits. The universally suitable present for a girl was a doll. It was bad luck if you didn't like them. The alternative was a tea set.

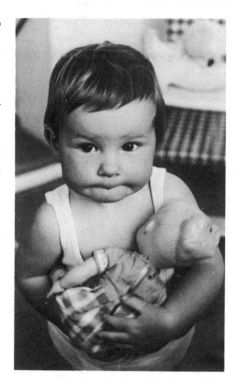

I love my dolly.

They gave rag dolls to babies which was ridiculous. By the time you were about three, they were putrid.

The awful thing about rag dolls was that their faces were painted on and they'd either rub off or fade. You'd be left with a one-eyed doll with half a mouth.

My grandmother used to make me peg dolls out of the old fashioned wooden pegs. They weren't exactly cuddly.

I remember the first proper doll I ever got. She had real nylon hair, her eyes opened and closed and she actually said Mumma. I gave her a bath and she never said Mumma or opened her eyes again. I felt like a murderer.

Everyone got a black doll. It had a scarf round its head and usually had a white spotted red dress.

I had a doll called Rosebud. She only had plastic hair, but I thought she was wonderful. I used to drag her round behind me, so she ended up with a snub nose.

My grandmother used to make my doll's clothes. She sat on the porch knitting and threading ribbons. "She needs a new cardigan," she'd say. Two hours later, the doll would have a new cardigan.

Every Christmas, I asked for a bride doll. My parents couldn't afford one, but finally, they got the money together. I took her down to the local sandpit to show her off. In the excitement, I left her there to go home for dinner. I went back and she was gone. It was devastating. This life long dream and I owned a bride doll for two hours.

Something for everyone.

The one present that boys and girls did share, was a watch. In terms of status, getting a watch was a monumental step forward. Watches didn't play music, do long multiplication or tell the time in New York. In fact, a second hand was a sign of technological sophistication.

The first watch I ever got lost ten minutes every hour. It didn't worry me. I just adjusted it. I thought it was the most wonderful thing I'd ever possessed.

I remember a girl who had a watch with "Swiss Made" printed in gold on the face. We were so envious. Nobody else had a Swiss watch.

You weren't allowed to "overwind" watches. I lived in mortal terror that I'd overwind mine and break it. It kept me constantly occupied.

My teacher confiscated my watch one day. I was too frightened to ask for it back, but I was terrified to go home without it. The first thing Mum asked every afternoon was "Did you lose your watch today?"

In general, girls had a much narrower range of toys than boys. As they got older, clothing items and books replaced dolls and tea sets. No-one ever thought of giving a girl Meccano or a train set. These were some of the most exciting, advanced toys of the era.

My cousin used to come down from Sydney after Christmas and bring his Meccano. With the two sets, you could make really extraordinary things. One year, we made a tower of London. Another year, we had the kit to make a clock, but we lost the cogs.

What I loved about Meccano were the different spanners and tools you got. One year, they put out a special little box to put tools in. It gave you a great feeling.

The red paint would wear off the Meccano pieces and sometimes the pieces would get a bit bent or warped. I was

And I made it myself.

Every boy had a trainset.

CARD GAMES

Snap
Old Maid
Strip Jack Naked
Mix and Match
Racing Patience
Patience
500
Pontoon
Canasta
Happy Families
Rickety Kate
Fish
Whist

always losing bits of mine. Most of my creations consisted of an incredible number of small pieces bolted together.

I got a chemistry set for my birthday. I wanted to use it, not read the instructions. I blew myself up on a fairly regular basis.

I got a chemistry set for my birthday because my parents thought it would help me develop an interest in science. I only wanted to make rotten egg gas.

A Hornby train set was the one to get. My brother's one actually had a light at the front of the train. We used to put a blanket over the window and watch it go round and round the track in the dark.

My brother and I had a great collection of Matchbox cars. I loved them, but we were quite fickle when we discovered friction cars. It was a great thing to have a car that actually went, and made a noise. With Matchbox cars you had to make your own vroooms and ne-oww noises.

Colouring In

Meccano, dolls, tea sets and cars were the 'big' toys. In addition, there were the smaller toys. These were part of everyday play equipment and an important part of childhood.

We did a lot of colouring in. There were always pictures in the Sunday papers to colour in and various competitions to go in for. If Mum thought we were bored, she would tell us to go and colour in.

My aunt once gave me a big set of Lakeland pencils, the ones that opened out like a fan. There were 144 colours. I used to spend a lot of time colouring in funny shades like "magenta 2" so the pencils would all end up the same length.

We had magic painting books that would colour in when you went over them with water. It was a fantastic idea, but in practice, the colours were all washed out or smudged.

The painting sets had little squares of paint. You could never get enough colour off them and when you opened them after a few weeks, they'd be all dried up and cracked.

Games for the Family

There were also the indoor games, sometimes played on rainy days after school, or on Saturday nights by the entire family. Before the advent of television, these indoor games were a more important part of family life. Children were usually familiar with a wide range of card games and board games.

Mum and I played "Snap" every night after tea. She would be shelling the peas for the next night at the same time, but she still used to beat me.

Getting our first set of Monopoly was incredibly exciting. We looked at the houses and the hotels. Then, we all sat down and actually counted out the money. We were half convinced it was real.

I could never get over the fact that my father cheated at Monopoly. He was so upright about everything else. If you caught him sliding on an extra square, he'd just roar with laughter. Cheating by an adult was incomprehensible to me then.

I played Snakes and Ladders for years, feeling as if I'd missed something. It took me ages to realise that what I was playing was actually all there was to it.

There was a game called "Fiddlesticks" which was just a lot of plastic sticks. You had to pick them up one by one without disturbing the others. It was really simple, but kids used to come round to our place because we were the family with the Fiddlesticks.

We used to play Scrabble every Saturday night, sitting round the dining room table. Mum kept score. At the end of every game she'd add up who got double scores and triple letters and divide our scores by our ages. We'd get paid according to our scores, but the little ones always got threepence and the older kids always got sixpence.

BOARD AND PAPER GAMES

Chess
Chinese Checkers
Twister
Ludo
Draughts
Snakes and Ladders
Jigsaw puzzles
Dominoes
Tiddlywinks
Hangman
Join the dots
Noughts and Crosses
Boxes
Bombers
Squares

The kitchen table doubled as the games table.

CHAPTER ELEVEN

Cocky Laura 1 2 3

Queenie, Queenie, who's got the ball?
Is she fat or is she small?
Is she thin or is she tall?
Queenie, Queenie, who's got the ball?

The Games we Played

The games of children are games with *rules*. In most childhood games, rules are the very essence of the game. The games and their rules are exclusive to children. No adult seriously plays hidings, or countries or poison ball. But each generation of children emulates and then modifies the games until the original is changed beyond recognition.

We played chasings with a vengeance, every lunchtime. When you were in, you counted up to ten, then you'd be off after the nearest fastest kid. You'd get her and she'd be in. Sometimes, if she was really slow, you'd get close and taunt her.

If you found a really good hiding place where no one could find you, everybody lost interest. They'd start playing something else. It was hollow victory.

I once hid under a friend's house. No one could find me and when I came out, one of the boys said that hiding in houses was out of bounds. We had a brawl over whether *under* houses was the same as *in* houses.

Cocky Laura 1 2 3 was a combination between chasings and hidings. When you got back to the bar [safe area], you had to shout out, "Cocky Laura 1 2 3". We had no idea what it meant. You never even thought about it.

I used to play "What's the time Mr Wolf?" with my older sister. When she got to high school, she disdained it. It was as if she had become a different person.

Many childhood games were based on capture and escape. It was survival of the fittest, with one child pitted against the rest. But once you had at least some captives on your team, there was an opportunity to disrupt the balance of power.

In "Red Rover Cross Over", you had to reach the other side of the playground without being caught by the person in the middle. If he caught you, you were on his team. Once the teams were more even, it got pretty hectic. Your shirt was likely to get ripped as you ran past. One kid smashed his teeth when he ran into the wall.

There were all sorts of catching games — British bulldog, releasings and others. Our headmaster banned them, one by one, because they always degenerated into brawls. Someone would end up with a broken arm and it'd be banned.

One of the scariest things when I was little was passwords. Boys would block off streets and wouldn't let you through unless you knew the password. You'd see other kids getting through. It felt like you'd never get home. If someone told you the password, they'd just change it.

Some games required equipment. It was usually nothing complex — an object that could be carried in a pocket, a ball, a taw, marbles or bottle tops. These items were very important personal possessions, seemingly endowed with magical properties.

The taw you had in hopscotch was terribly important. People had bits of glass or bathroom tiles. I had a bit of white quartz, really smooth. I could rely on it to go just where I wanted. I left it on the hopscotch one day and the next day a girl claimed she'd found one exactly like it. Everyone was on my side, but she wouldn't give it back.

MARBLE MEMORIES

Connie agates
Clay dibs
Cat eyes
Steelies (ballbearings)
Alleys
Blood alleys
Tom Bowlers
Blood bath

Marbles was a betting game.

I had a blood alley marble that I'd won. It was my lucky marble. I used to lie in bed at night and look at it. One day I bet it against a whole lot of connie agates. It was one of those stupid bets you just don't understand. I offered the kid the rest of my marbles, but he wanted the blood alley. It was like giving a pound of flesh.

Knuckles was a really big craze. Most of us had real knuckle bones. We were in awe when one of the girls got coloured plastic ones from her aunt in the city. They were the *real* thing.

We used to collect bottle tops. You'd get a line of them on your arm and then toss them against the wall. It was important to get the right bottle tops.

You'd get empty cigarette packets, fold them into cards and flick them. There was a lot of skill in the folding. They were better when they'd been folded a while and smoothed out.

Ball Games

Tennis balls, cricket balls, footballs, basketballs are part of the essential equipment of childhood. They are at the basis of many informal games. Ball skills are vital for social survival.

There was a complicated ritual of throwing a tennis ball up against a wall. It went one to ten. One was just throwing and catching. Two was single-handed with your right hand, three with your left, four under the left leg, five under the right, six turning around, seven turning round twice. Ten was probably doing a cartwheel in between throws.

When the ball against the wall games came round, I was really popular. We had a concrete drive and the house didn't have many windows on that side. There would be ten kids every afternoon, throwing balls against the house for a couple of hours. Mum said it was like living in a ballbearing factory.

We used to play French cricket in the middle of the road on summer nights. All the kids from the neighbourhood came and it'd be dead serious. Then, a car would come round the corner and scatter us. We'd fight and argue about exactly where the batsman had been and how close the bowler had really got.

In "countries", you'd throw the ball up really high and everyone would have to run away until you'd called out a country. The person whose country it was had to run back and catch it. If they didn't, they were out. Being Italy was considered very unlucky for some reason.

Poison ball was really vicious. You were all in a circle and if the person on the outside hit you on the leg below the knee, you'd have to go to the outside of the circle. Once you got a few people on the outside, it was really hard and fast. When you got hit, you got a big red mark on your leg.

Look Mum! I can Fly

Superheroes were the basis of many games. Tarzan, Superman, the Phantom and others all provided inspiration. Cowboys and Indians appealed to the gang mentality of children and was always popular.

Having the right gear was important.

My worst memories of cowboys and Indians was of actually being hung. I was an Indian and the cowboys took it fairly seriously.

It was always a bit more prestigious being a cowboy. But I took great pride in being the chief of an Indian tribe that actually ran our suburb for a few years.

Girls weren't allowed to play. My brother said I couldn't make the gun noises properly. I thought it was something inherently different about girls.

If you shot someone, you yelled, "Take you death." They'd stagger round, then pretend to recover. It was infuriating.

I tied our passionfruit vine around a branch of the camphor laurel and tried to do a Tarzan down it. All that came down were a lot of green passionfruit.

We couldn't afford proper Superman capes. We used to wear our singlets flapping behind us and whoosh up and down the footpath.

Nobody ever believed their mother that you couldn't fly by jumping off the garage roof. It was one of those things all mothers said.

After coming off the garage roof a couple of times, I almost accepted I couldn't fly. But one night I had this dream I could fly, just a couple of inches off the road. I flew up to the lights at Bexley Road and back again. It was real close to the ground, but it was flying. It was so vivid I was convinced it was possible.

Crazy Crazes

While boys dominated the world of the superheroes, it was largely the girls who started the fads and the crazes. Without warning, these would sweep through suburbs, generating intense, obsessive and unremitting activity.

Skipping ropes would appear from nowhere. We never had ones with proper handles, just bits of rope. But it was very

You thought you really could fly.

important that they were the right weight and length. You knew the season was coming to an end when your rope started getting stringy at the bottom.

I begged Dad to get me a long rope at the hardware shop. It stretched right across the road and you'd get a whole line of girls running in, until everyone was skipping.

My friend and I practised doing doubles until we were perfect. We stood, facing each other, skipping, for hours. It was quite a feat because I was 6 inches taller than her.

My mother wouldn't give me a piece of elastic when the elastic craze started. She said it was a waste. I hated her because I was always the one at the end holding the elastic out with my feet.

As the season got on, the elastics would become longer and longer and need more and more people. You couldn't cross the playground without tripping over an elastic.

I can remember my first hula hoop craze. I thought they were the first hula hoops in the whole world.

The hoops were made out of bamboo and you could tell which was yours by the colour of the rattan binding.

The trick was to start the hoop round your waist, take it down your legs, work it up to your chest, then round your neck, then down one arm. It was all done with no hands. Then you had to do all that walking along.

The wool you used for the cat's cradle craze was very important. It had to be thick enough so you could see the final

A healthy obsession.

result, but not too thick to get tangled up or furry. I had a fantastic bit of blue wool, but it got confiscated.

I'd just learnt to do the cup and saucer under the desk. The teacher saw what I was doing and snatched it away. I asked for it back later, and she said, "That stupid thing, I threw it in the bin." I was mortified.

There were farmer's gate, cat's cradle, parachute, the church and best of all, the Sydney Harbour Bridge.

With swap cards, a person was worth two of a landscape, unless the person was a soldier or some other man. Then, a landscape was worth two of the person. You used the patterns at the back and the front to keep the rest clean.

My grandmother sent me three jokers from her playing cards. They were pictures of the same woman — one with a pink scarf, one with a green scarf, one with a yellow scarf. Everybody was really jealous.

My friend had a card with an angel, with wings, a halo and a frilly dress. She was surrounded by clouds and flowers. There was a castle in the background. I thought it was the most beautiful thing I'd ever seen, but she wouldn't swap it for anything.

May there be just enough clouds in your life to form a glorious sunset

Make new friends
But keep the old.
New ones are silver
Old ones are gold.

The thing was to be able to go through your cards very fast. You kept them in order of merit, with patterns at the back.

I thought, I thought,
I thought in vain
At last I thought
I'd write my name

When autograph books came in, you'd imagine having all sorts of famous people in your book. All you ever got were uncles and aunties and friends. It was really grotty to get your parents' autograph, or your brother's.

You let your best friend write on a pink page.

Kind hearts are gardens
Kind thoughts are roots
Kind words are flowers
Kind deeds are fruits

A boy took my book and wrote "BUM" on it. I was devastated. It had been so beautiful up until then.

Everyone would be finger knitting, all through playtime and lunchtime. We were always short of wool.

This page is like a cabbage patch
Where every goose must have a scratch
So must I

My friend and I finger-knitted a piece that went right around the block. After that, we ran out of steam.

. . . .
(signature)

We knitted through cotton reels with four nails at the top. The trouble with that was that if you made a mistake, you didn't see it till it came out the other end of the reel.

Pompoms were a miracle to me. I could make them but I didn't understand how they materialised. The trouble was you'd end up with fifty pompoms and no use for them at all.

Yoyos were big time, because they were American.

The Coca Cola yoyos weren't only reputed to be better, they really were better. You could actually do all those things like walk the dog and spin the hat. It was a whole new technology.

I used to practise and practise. The only thing I could ever do was get it to go up and down the string. *And* the string kept getting tangled.

Eeny Meeny Miney Mo

Decisions were frequently made by the quaint custom of baggsing. 'I baggs it!' and you had it. Rhymes were also part of the conventional decision-making processes of childhood. They were used to decide who had first turn. They could also determine who took the dare to walk along the fence or who took their pants off. Some, like 'Step on a crack and you'll marry a black' were purely cautionary. Many were racist.

Ickey ackey 'orses cackey,
What colour will it be?
Yellow. . . .
Y..E..L..L..O..W

Eeny, meeny, miney, mo,
Catch a nigger by the toe.
If he hollers let him go,
Eeeny, meeny, miney mo.

One potato, two potato, three potato four.
Five potato, six potato, seven potato more!

Rhymes used in games such as skipping and hopscotch were often more complex. In skipping, they were used to time when you went in, and to pace the skippers.

I went to a Chinese restaurant
To buy a loaf of bread
He wrapped it up in a ten bob note
And this is what he said:
Eli eli,
Chickabye, chickabye,
Saw a sausage,
In bed.
Went to the other one,
Got me another one
Do me a favour,
Drop dead!

I saw Esau sitting on a see-saw,
I saw Esau sitting on a gate.
I saw Esau sitting on a see-saw,
I saw Esau kissing Kate.

Half a pound of tuppeny rice,
Half a pound of treacle,
That's the way the money goes,
Pop goes the weasel.

After the Profumo scandal, this was changed to:

Half a pound of Mandy Rice,
Half a pound of Keeler,
Put 'em together and what have you got?
One sexy sheila!

Private Games

Although most games were bound by rules and conventions, there were the more private, individual games, often played within a family. They had an intensity and pleasure all of their own.

My brother would play and I would make up songs for us to sing.

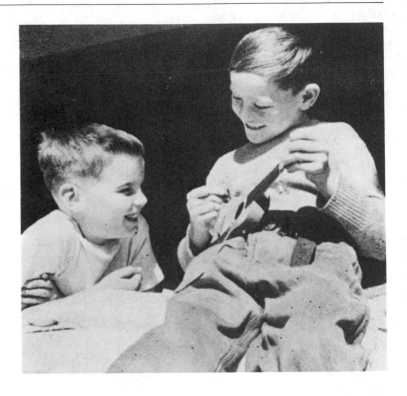

We danced on the lawn at night. We climbed out the window after we'd all been put to bed and just danced. Sometimes, if we were feeling brave, we'd run round the block in the dark.

We had pine trees down the bottom of the paddock. They were only half grown. We'd each climb a tree and hang on, as they shook in the wind.

There were sandhills behind the beach. Sometimes I went up there by myself and slid down, really slowly. It was as if the earth was moving under me.

I used to go down the bush by myself. I'd pretend I was a dog. I ran through the bush panting.

My brother and I had a barrel. One of us would get in and the other would roll it down the drive. You were spinning round and round in a frenzy of noise until you finally crashed into the garage door.

We had a family tradition called a "shompong". We'd all sit on the bed and bounce and call out "shompong, shompong".

CHAPTER TWELVE

Wheels

Knock, knock,
Who's there?
Isabelle.
Isabelle who?
Is a bell necessary on a bike?

Wonderful Wheels

In the post-war period, bikes were one of the most important and exciting possessions for any child. Even the much maligned tricycle gave a certain amount of independence and provided an entree to footpath society. But the real status symbol was the two-wheeler, a prized possession, not bestowed lightly by parents. For many years, the bike manufacturers did not make bikes for very small children. There were no trainer wheels. Until the age of at least six or seven, children rode tricycles or scooters.

The trikes were quite big and solid. They always had a deep tin tray on the back. In the ads (or in your mother's imagination) there was always a teddy bear or a doll in it. In real life, you shoved your little sister or your cat in and pedalled like hell so they couldn't get out.

The worst thing about the tricycles were the old tin seats. They had nails coming through, or rough bits of tin. It was like sitting on a badly opened can.

Even on a trike, you could get up quite a speed going down hill. The only trouble was that you couldn't keep your feet on the pedals because they were going so fast.

We had one of those pedal cars. It looked great. Other kids were really envious, but in fact, you couldn't do much with it.

We were proud of our first tricycles. What's more, you didn't need a licence.

We couldn't afford a tricycle, so we used the old pram. You'd stand on the bar at the front and sort of scoot along. Visibility wasn't real good because we couldn't get the hood down.

My brother would put me in the pram and run me down the hill. There was a main road at the bottom. Every single time he'd promise not to let go. Every single time he did.

Push Power

A scooter was a step up from a tricycle, although it didn't have quite the status of the much coveted two-wheeler. Nevertheless, unlike the tricycle, it wasn't immediately discarded when the two-wheeler finally made its appearance.

I desperately wanted a scooter, one of the English ones with the blow-up tyres. I wanted it so much that I created an imaginary one. Whenever it rained, I'd rush outside to rescue the imaginary scooter. I'd walk round, pushing it along with one leg. My parents finally bought me one. I was terribly disappointed. It didn't have pneumatic tyres like the one in my head.

We had a good English scooter with tyres so you didn't get thrown off at every bump in the footpath. The best thing was that you could fit three kids on it.

We had a really cheap and nasty scooter. It didn't have tyres or a brake and it clunked along. But you could get up to a fantastic speed on a good downhill run. It skewed to one side, so you had to know how to handle it. Otherwise you'd end up on the nature strip and mow down the agapanthus.

Pedal Power

One of the best and most memorable of all childhood presents was the long awaited two-wheeler. Unlike even the best of scooters, the bike was a real, adult, form of transport. In this lay much of the magic for children. In Melbourne, the two-wheeler had to be a Malvern Star, in Sydney, a Speedwell. The two-wheeler immediately

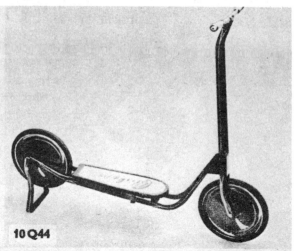

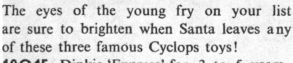

The eyes of the young fry on your list are sure to brighten when Santa leaves any of these three famous Cyclops toys!
10Q45: Dinkie 'Express' for 3 to 5 years. Balanced to prevent tipping. 13 *lbs.* **83/6**

10Q44: Cyclops scooter for boy or girl, 5-9 years. Foot operated rear brake. 14 *lbs.* **89/6**
10Q43 (*right*): Red frame tandem bike; white wheels and blue seat. Small back seat for extra passenger. 4 to 7 years. 20 *lbs.* **£9/19/6**

replaced the three-wheeler, the world of 'little kids' left behind forever.

I woke up in the middle of the night before my birthday. It was pitch black but I could *feel* the bike beside my bed. I actually tried to do a turn round my room and ended up crashing into the cupboard. It was my first bike accident.

I told my parents I wanted a Malvern Star, green with gold stars. It was the year of the Olympic Games in Melbourne and I felt very patriotic. We all had hand-me-down bikes, even for Christmas, but Dad had painted my older sister's dark green and did the stars in gold. I got that and she got Mum's old 26 inch done in maroon, with gold stars. To us, they were new bikes.

I desperately wanted a new 26 inch. I thought I'd be getting a real super dooper one. It looked okay, but it had "Parramatta Reconditioned" written down the side. My parents had scrimped and saved to buy it, but I still felt really ashamed of not having a *new* bike.

Bike ownership conferred membership of an elite. It was an elite to which almost everyone eventually belonged. Within the bike riding fraternity, there were, of course various levels to be aspired to. Girls, for instance, rarely aspired to a racing bike. A pink cane basket on the front was a female status symbol. Little kids wanted plastic streamers and loud bells. The sophisticates coveted gears and lights. A front pedal brake in addition to the back pedal brake was useful if the chain broke. While such things were important, speed and skill were paramount.

You needed a kid with a watch for the speed trials. We used to go down the hill, round the shops and up — all "on your honour". Dad brought home an old bike with gears and I was convinced I could thrash them. I put it into first because I thought that would be fastest. I struggled up the hill, not understanding how it could be so hard, somehow convinced I *must* be going fast.

We used to ride on the road and do a neat dodge in and out of the cars. My father told me he'd take the bike off me if he saw me doing it again. I can still remember how furious I was, seeing it hanging up on the verandah for weeks and weeks.

We'd link arms and ride abreast. You'd get about six kids joined up, and then you'd come to the corner. There'd be a car coming and you'd all freak.

Long before BMX bikes we were jumping gutters and going through puddles. We tried to jump the creek. About half the kids would land in there with bits of bike coming out their ears.

We had really elaborate courses that you had to ride — up driveways, under hoses, round things and over flowerbeds. We weren't popular with the local gardeners.

The great thing was the freedom. Just get on and go. We'd ride for miles. You'd find places you'd never see otherwise. You'd get a bit panicky when the street lights came on, wondering if you could find your way home before it got really dark.

Pegging a cigarette card to the spokes made a terrific clicking, whirring sound. Everybody knew where you were.

You'd dink your mate to school, sometimes on the front,

sometimes on the back. It was a real mate's thing to do, so he wouldn't have to be one of the kids that walked.

Walking Wounded

Bike repair was a constant feature of bike riding — pumping up tyres, fixing punctures, using a bucket of water to detect the holes, tightening brakes and adjusting the chain. Most suburbs supported a bike shop which did more complex repairs. Bikes suffered all forms of abuse. The casualty rate amongst riders was fairly high, although they were mostly walking wounded. Young children were exhorted not to ride on the road. Older children were frequently credited with sense they didn't possess.

Back pedal brakes often just gave out. You had to press your heel up against the back tyre when you wanted to stop. It was pretty hairy coming down a steep hill with bare feet.

I loved going down the hill full speed and sticking my feet out. Unfortunately, I'd catch them on a fence and come home broken and bleeding, carrying the bike. My parents would rush round, doing minor surgery on my cuts and bruises and I'd be yelling at them to fix the bike.

The seat came off the three-wheeler. There was just a lethal looking spike left there. Dad put it away in the garage with strict instructions that no-one — not anyone — was to get onto it. On Saturday morning when the family went shopping, I got it out. Because there was no seat, there was no way I could pedal, so I stood on the tray at the back and pushed off down the hill. It was totally out of control in about two seconds. I chose to crash into the lamp-post rather than on the road. I ended up with a broken arm.

My worst bike accident was when I got my ear hooked on a bridge post.

Billycart Mayhem

If bikes were a health hazard, billycarts were even more so. They were designed and built purely for speed, with no regard for safety.

The first billycart was an old fruit box on pram wheels. We were only very little when we made it. We didn't realise you couldn't actually nail wood to metal. In the "she'll be right" tradition, it split into several pieces on its first downhill trial.

My brother made and designed his own. The first was made with old bike wheels. It looked like a wheelchair. We were laughed off the street.

You got a fantastic noise with ballbearings. With all the neighbourhood kids coming down the hill, it sounded like a motorised army.

We had a great hill for billycarting. The main road at the bottom seemed irrelevant.

Dinking your little sister home from the shops.

Any old box could be the basis of a billycart.

We were the billycart champions. We thought people who had brakes were dopes. They just slowed you down.

CHAPTER THIRTEEN

Under Construction

Captain Cook was a brave man,
He sailed the ocean in a frying pan.

Learning by Experience

For many years, parents provided toys for children and left them to their own devices. Then educationalists hit on the idea that children learnt through play. Thus, the kindergarten movement of the 1920s and 1930s was born. In the post-war era, this was embraced with renewed enthusiasm. Mothers were exhorted to encourage children in creative, constructive play. Blocks, sandpits and finger painting were acceptable activities. However, what started in the sandpit did not necessarily translate directly into educational achievement.

I was a sandpit child. The next step was tunnelling. I was very proud of the tunnel I was digging towards the back door. Then Dad stood on it and it caved in. He sprained his ankle. Henceforth, tunnelling was strictly forbidden.

My brother was heavily into tunnelling and I was fascinated by graveyards. We shared the digging. He could crawl through the tunnels, but we had a few side passages. They were graves for my old dolls.

We found some bones when we were digging. We were convinced they were human remains and took them to the museum. Unfortunately, they were lamb shanks.

Our road was unsealed so when it rained we had torrents rushing down it. We constructed elaborate earthworks, dams and great channels. It looked like a tribe of beavers lived there.

We'd make boats out of leaves and sticks and then send them off down the drain. We'd rush down the street to see them come out again. They hardly ever did.

Treehouses

Construction work eventually moved out of the primeval slime onto a higher plane. However, there was a high casualty rate when it came to treehouses.

I fell and caught the under side of my arm on a nail. I ripped my whole arm open. I was a lot more careful where I put the nails after that.

Getting the timber was the hard bit. You'd go and nonchalantly lean up against someone's fence. As you walked away, you'd actually rip the piece of paling off. You tried to walk as if it was attached to you. You'd tell your mother you found it.

I spent days making a treehouse with my mate. It seemed secure and solid. We were really proud of it. We went over one side to admire the view. The whole thing tilted gently over on a forty five degree angle and we ended up in the backyard.

Mum used to come after me. I'd run straight out the back door and then straight up the sloping trunk of the Camphor Laurel. Once I was up there, I was safe.

Water Craft

Construction also ran to vehicles and craft of various kinds. An even more elusive dream than the treehouse, was the possibility of escape on water.

My first boat was made of two sheets of corrugated tin and wire. With a mate, I hammered the tin out flat and then joined it together with the wire. It sank immediately. We realised the problem was that it wasn't waterproof, so we collected melting tar from the road and plugged up all the holes. We paddled right out into the bay. Eventually, it started to leak so we paddled back in. We could see the bottom splitting open, but we were near the shore. The actual split occurred right in the middle of a congestion of blue bottles.

I'd been making boats for years, without any success, when fibreglass came on the market. I was sure it was the answer to my prayers. I was convinced I'd finally get something that floated. It did — upside down.

We'd always wanted to make a raft, so we wouldn't have to walk all the way round by the road. We made one out of planks and tyres and chains. It was very seaworthy, but it was so heavy that it was quicker going round by the road.

Cubbyhouses

If trees and boats were the preserve of boys, cubby construction was dominated by girls. It was an approved activity, thought to encourage domestic instincts.

We always had cubbies at school, down in the bushy part. The trick was to get a good spot. You had to fight for it. Then you put sandstones round it. We swept the dirt floor, and tied bits of material on the tree branches for curtains. Once the cubbies got too elaborate, the headmaster would make us dismantle them. A couple of months later, we'd start building up again.

We had a cubby down in the bush. It was an old Post Office box made of tin which had been used to carry coils of wire. The boys were always raiding us, but we held our ground.

We girls had a cubby up the back behind the woodshed. One day my sister decided we'd have a fire to keep warm. It set the woodshed on fire.

I had a cubby under my bed. I told my sister a red fox lived there. I convinced myself more than her. I'd lie in bed at night, terrified, thinking of the fox in the cubby under there.

Indoor Construction

The ultimate in cubby houses was the prepackaged variety.

Construction embraced not only tunnels, treehouses, boats and cubbies, but various other inside hobbies and craft. Some were more productive than others.

I spent all my pocket money on balsa wood and glue. I had a fantastic penknife and I'd spend hours working away at little model planes. In fact, they got littler and littler and littler, until there was more Tarzan's Grip than wood.

I made a fantastic Tiger Moth model — my best ever. The only problem was that it was stuck very firmly to the dining room table. My mother *had* told me to put down newspaper.

I was very jealous of all the things the boys made. My mother used to say, "Never mind, we'll cut out some paper dolls." Yuk!

I could never get the paper dolls holding hands. I made the ones with the double hips.

You'd get books of doll's clothes to cut out, with little paper tabs to fold over the dolls. Some of them were fantastic, but the tabs always broke.

I loved plaster of Paris moulds. Unfortunately, I was always too impatient and I peeled off the rubber before they set. I had a very big collection of animals without ears or with missing legs.

One day Dad showed us how to make stilts with jam tins and strings. There weren't enough matching jam tins. I got an uneven pair, but they still worked.

We made telephones with Ardmona peach tins and string tied through the bottom. You'd say something to the person at the other end and then scream out, "Can you hear me?"

I was really intrigued by a kit which said you could make a crystal radio in a cigarbox. Dad got it for me and we somehow got it together. It worked, but I was really disappointed. There was no way you could fit it in a cigarbox.

I made a crystal radio from a kit and had wires going out the window, up into trees. I picked up a lot of static with the odd

It was easier with help from a friend.

word you could hear every few minutes. I lay in bed at night, listening to it for hours.

In wet weather, Mum would get out all the old Christmas cards and birthday cards. We made paste out of flour and water, cut out the cards and stuck them into scrapbooks. They were for children in hospital. But we never sent them because the paste never dried properly or the pages got stuck together.

We made kites on rainy days. We used old fruit boxes and brown paper and made the tails from newspaper. Mostly, they didn't even get off the ground.

Cooking up a Storm

Make and do extended to the kitchen, where there were a limited number of things children were allowed to make.

We were really excited about getting a ginger beer plant then terribly disappointed when we saw it. I thought it'd be some sort of plant with ginger beer hanging off it. It was just grey mush. But it did get exciting when the bottles started exploding in the middle of the night. It sounded like a round of gunfire.

My mother who was a strict teetotaler, encouraged the boys to make a raspberry cordial. It must have fermented and they were all falling about drunk. Mother was very naive. To her, it was proof you really could be happy without alcohol.

Mum used to let us make our own honeycomb with golden syrup and bicarb of soda. It was stickier than a Violet Crumble bar, and it lasted longer.

The first time we made chocolate crackles I was amazed at how such a fantastic food was so easy to make.

Scavengers

Rubbish days were events put on by local councils. Every household put its rubbish on the nature strip for

Chocolate Crackles
4 cups of rice bubbles
1½ cups of sifted icing sugar
3 tablespoons of sifted cocoa
1 cup of desiccated coconut
8 ounces of melted copha

Combine rice bubbles, icing sugar, cocoa and coconut in a mixing bowl. Add the copha, slightly cooled and mix well. Spoon into patty cake containers.

collection. Children assiduously picked over the rubbish and took it home. The exercise thus turned into one of recycling rather than disposing of neighbourhood rubbish.

I got an old wire bed frame. I had great ambitions of making a Hills Hoist for Mum. We threw it out the next year.

I dragged home an old cot. Mum said, "But we don't have a baby." I didn't have an answer to that.

We were always looking for ballbearings for billycarts. Sometimes, you'd get them on the dumps, but mostly you had to beg at local garages. There were never enough.

We'd go through the rubbish and get the old clothes for dress ups. The neighbours hated you trailing round in their old nighties.

My Mum used to cut down the old clothes and make up proper dress-up clothes. We were the only kids who had them.

CHAPTER FOURTEEN

Dead Tadpoles and Other Animals

Roses are red,
Violets are blue.
I've got a bulldog,
That looks like you.

A Dog's Life!

The days of designer dogs are comparatively recent. In the post-war years, exotics such as Afghans, Old English Sheepdogs and Basset Hounds were rarely seen on the streets. Pekinese were kept by old ladies. Fox Terriers were popular as pets and bad-tempered Corgis were kept in deference to the Queen. Cattledogs were nasty dogs kept by nasty people. Most family mutts had a dash of Kelpie in addition to other bits and pieces. They were not named after eastern mystics or pop stars, but were given simple names like 'Spot', 'Rover' or 'Tag'. Dogs were allowed on the street. Any self-respecting dog chased cars as well as taking an occasional nip out of the local kids on bikes.

We had a mad dog called Harry, who believed his job in life was to round up a flock of kids on bikes. It drove him mad because he never got it together.

My dog Flossie went everywhere with me — to the park, to the bush, up to the shops. Everyone knew her. When she got run over, it was the saddest day of my life, much worse than when my grandmother died.

Blackie was born the same year I was. She only had one and a half legs because she had a thing about rabbit traps.

We had a great dog called "Skipper". Unfortunately, he bit the local policeman. That was the end of him. He'd never bitten anyone else.

Nobody really minded dogs having puppies.

121

Veterinary care was a luxury that many people could not afford. Frequently, a trip to the vet meant destruction for the animal. Less robust animals lingered on, never sick, never well.

We seemed to have a series of dogs with runny eyes, bad breath or mange. You'd get a dog, think it would be okay and then it'd die.

Mum used to get hysterical about sick dogs. She'd scream at us not to touch them — we'd catch something dreadful.

Our headmaster felt called upon to give a lecture on rabies. It was very graphic. No-one felt very comfortable when we got out of school and found the usual troop of dogs waiting for us.

Mum used to send me on messages to the sewing lady round the corner. She had a mad Kelpie which had a thing about little girls. It'd be hanging onto your leg for dear life. The sewing lady would be talking about turning the edge on sheets. I'd be dragging this sex-crazed thing down the hall. She'd pretend she didn't notice.

We had a mad randy dog. Mum was so embarrassed she pretended not to notice. Then one day she couldn't stand it any more and got him put down.

Cats' Tales

Cats were as common as dogs. They were less delinquent, except in their breeding habits.

I was horrified when I found my father drowning kittens. I couldn't believe it. Here was my nice kind Dad behaving as if murder was an everyday event.

We named our cat Pelaco because he had a white shirt.

We heard a cat always landed on its feet, whatever height it fell from. We experimented with our cat Smokey. It was true.

We had an extremely patient cat. We dressed him in doll's clothes, took him for rides on the back of the dinky and made him treehouses. The only time he rebelled was when we tried to give him a bath.

Creatures Great and Small

Angora rabbits were the ultimate.

Parents who refused to have a dog or a cat could sometimes be persuaded to have a smaller mammal — a guineapig, rabbit or mouse. Failing that, many children had a budgie, or, at least, a goldfish.

The trouble with guineapigs was that they could only do one thing — make more guineapigs.

We had a rabbit called Hoppy, not because he hopped, but after Hop-along Cassidy.

I was devoted to my rabbit. One day the dog got him. I came home and he was was in bits all over the lawn. Mass murder with one rabbit.

The trouble about rabbits is they poo so much. Ours used to hop round the verandah leaving a trail with each hop.

Dad made the mice a wonderful cage. The wood was too soft and they gnawed their way out. We couldn't catch them. One was living in the kitchen. Mum was terrific. She refused to set a trap.

I liked the mouse at first. Then I had to clean out the cage. I was so disgusted I let it go. Everybody said what a shame it had escaped, but they were relieved too.

We had a budgie who talked brilliantly. "Hullo . . . how are you today . . . nice day." He sounded really friendly. But when you got near the cage, he'd rip your hand off.

We had a cockatoo that went bald. It was really creepy. I never admitted to anyone I had him.

Mum used to put the budgie out in the sun once a week because that's what you were supposed to do. The southerly came up and he ended up, cage and all, three doors down.

Living in a flat, we only had a goldfish. I used to look at him and dream he was a whale.

I told my friend I'd trained my goldfish. I said I'd taught him to jump over a piece of wool. Then I said he wouldn't do it in front of other people. It was one of those lies you begin to believe yourself.

Wildlife in Suburbia

More exciting than goldfish were the annual tadpole catching excursions. The tadpoles bred in creeks and bush pools or in water at rubbish dumps. Jam jars and stocking nets were important equipment. In cases of emergency, tadpoles were taken home, hand held.

Somebody would say there were tadpoles in the creek and we'd all be down there with jars and nets. It was a hierarchy. The biggest kids got the most tadpoles.

We'd get the tadpoles home and Mum would say, "But where are you going to keep them?" We'd always promise to build a proper aquarium, but they always died off before we got round to it.

A couple of the tadpoles would die, and you'd know the rest were on the way out.

I thought all the tadpoles were dead and I left the jar out in the shed. I went back weeks later and there was this frog floating on the top, all blue and bloated. I felt very guilty.

I felt so excited when I saw them growing legs. We put them in a shallow dish so they could rest on the edge. The next morning they were all gone.

One year I got one frog to take back to the creek. In all those years, it was the sole survivor.

If frogs performed poorly in the domestic setting, silkworms also led a precarious life. But despite casualties, generation after generation survived.

If you had a mulberry tree, you were very popular in the silkworm season.

The hardest thing about getting the silkworms was finding a shoebox.

I kept my silkworms in my lunch box for a week. My mother was disgusted.

You could feed them rose leaves and they spun red silk.

I saw myself in a silk dressing-gown, with silk stockings. But I couldn't get the silk off the cocoon.

I often felt really guilty about my silkworms. I forgot about them when they'd spun the cocoon. I'd look at the box months later and there would be the dead moths and some eggs.

The dog kept a tally of the tadpoles.

The life cycle of cicadas also presented a mystery. Some years, summer would buzz with cicadas. Other years,

CICADAS

Yellow Mondays
Green Grocer
Black Prince
Cherry Nose
Double Drummer
Floury Miller
Frenchy

there would be almost none. More than other insects, cicadas played an important part in childhood. There were all the different varieties to be caught. They were non-poisonous and were easily handled.

Mum would never let us keep cicadas. I put one in a box under my bed. At midnight, it started drumming. It was a double drummer and it woke the whole house up.

You'd watch the birds catch them in mid-flight and peck off the end. They'd keep flying for a while and then come down, all the body gone.

We'd watch them come out of their shells. It looked really painful, but if you tried to help they really got into a mess.

I collected 200 cicada shells one Christmas. I was sure someone would find a use for them.

Chook Chook Chook

As well as its regulation Hills Hoist, almost every backyard had a chook house. Before the days of landscaping, pergolas and swimming pools, backyards were places for kids to play, to dry the washing, grow vegetables and keep chooks. The chook yard, mundane in its function, did provide some childhood dramas.

The dog would get in and kill a chook. Dad would threaten to kill the dog. The chooks would stop laying and Mum would threaten to kill the chooks. When rats got up in the chook yard, Dad went off his head about the next door's chooks having lice and attracting rats. It got so you were scared of collecting the eggs.

The chook mash was pollet and bran mixed with warm water. I used to eat it.

The chooks would find a secret place to lay. Then one day the egg would explode and everything stank.

That sour chook manure smell. Revolting.

Mum used to like the chooks and have names for them. I could never understand how anyone could like a chook.

I couldn't eat the eggs if they were warm. I always made Mum cook a cold one from the fridge.

When my brother went off to boarding school, I was next in line to kill a chook. My father made it look easy. But when it was my turn, the chook wouldn't keep its head on the chopping block. I put my foot on its head and nearly cut my foot off. The chook was still alive. Finally, I took a swipe and cut its head straight down the middle. It winked at me with its remaining eye.

Mum would always say, "Take the scraps out for Socrates." He was our pet duck, but we had killed him for Christmas dinner. It was a bit bleak, but no-one said anything during the meal. Then Mum said, "Take the scraps out to . . ." and burst into tears. It hit home what we'd done.

Creepy Crawlies

Besides the odd bad-tempered dog, there were other dangerous animals. Bull ants, soldier ants, ticks, spiders and even snakes were a threat not to be ignored. Happily, the battle was more than evenly matched.

I felt very vindictive towards bull ants. We'd find a nest and squash the black bits off as many ants as we could. I'd only been bitten once.

The worst thing was at school, eating your lunch and a bull ant got down your sock. It always bit you when you were killing it.

We'd block up the soldier ants' nests with tar from the road. They weren't as bad as bull ants, but they were pretty bad.

We were always on the look out for funnel webs. We spent our summers in fear of funnel webs. We never saw one.

My mother used to pick up tarantulas in her bare hands and take them outside. She wouldn't let us kill them.

Better dead than alive.

Redbacks went with outside dunnies. It was the thought of getting bitten on the bum.

We heard of a girl in Tasmania who got bitten on the bum by a snake. She died because she was too embarrassed to have anyone suck the poison out. It made sense to me. I would have rather died.

We lived in the suburbs, but there was still enough bush around to worry about snakes. I remember I used to run through the bushy parts to school. I thought they lay in wait for you.

We had a big chart of all the snakes up in the classroom. Our headmaster used to tell us how he could crack snakes like a whip. None of us believed him, but it was a very vivid picture.

Whenever we went down the bush, Mum would go through our hair when we came back. If we had any ticks, she'd put metho on them and pull them out.

Why is a snake so smart?
Because you can't pull its leg.

It was supposed to be worse to pull the body off and leave the tick head in. The head by itself would burrow right in to your heart and kill you.

I missed a tick one night. I got terribly sick with vomiting and a headache. The next morning they found the tick under my arm.

The dog would begin to drag his back legs and Mum would say, "Quick, up to the vet." In the end, one killed him.

Inky, pinky, ponky,
Daddy bought a donkey.
Donkey died.
Daddy cried.
Inky, pinky, ponky.

Animals on Show

There were no animal liberationists to induce guilty qualms in children going to the zoo or the circus. These excursions, before the days of wildlife television documentaries, provided a mixture of wonderment and pity.

Chooks didn't win prizes but goats did.

The elephant is a dainty bird,
It hops from bough to bough.
It settles in a rhubarb tree,
And whistles like a cow.

I was really horrified when I saw the polar bear. The concrete was painted green, but it was really hot and his fur looked yellow.

I could not believe that the giraffe could pee for so long. It went on and on and on. My mother got very embarrassed and tried to pull us away. We talked about it for months afterwards.

I was dropping broken biscuits into the elephant's trunk. Suddenly he sneezed. A mixture of elephant snot and biscuit sprayed everywhere.

The lions looked so depressed. It was my first circus, a big treat, but I cried all through it.

The elephant ride was really disappointing. You just swayed a bit, but it felt quite safe. I thought it'd be like Mowgli in the *Jungle Books.*

After seeing the dogs at the circus, I felt really disappointed with my dog. I made him wear my tutu, but he sat there and looked persecuted.

CHAPTER FIFTEEN

Saturday Flicks

Tarzan swing, Tarzan swear,
Tarzan rips his underwear
Tarzan say, me no care,
Jane make me another pair.

The Matinee

Saturday afternoon at the movies combined almost every social need of the Australian child of the 1940s, 1950s and 1960s. It provided a meeting place, entertainment and food, all exclusively for children. No adults in their right mind would go to see the *Adventures of Bugs Bunny* or the continuing thrills and spills of *Tarzan* swinging through the jungle.

Every Saturday afternoon of my childhood, I went to the movies. I caught the tram down the hill with my brother. All the kids on the tram were going down to the Odeon. If someone wasn't there, you knew they were sick.

There was a frenzy of activity outside. We always brought a stack of comics to swap. *Bugs Bunny* for *Superman*. *Mickey Mouse* for the *Phantom*. It was an important part of going to the movies.

Mum gave us two bob each. She told us to go upstairs. The seats upstairs were one and threepence. Downstairs, they were elevenpence. If we went upstairs, we could still get a Jersey Bar each.

We couldn't afford to buy lollies. Mum made us honeycomb to take. It was good, but I always wanted a proper Violet Crumble.

What did Tarzan say when he saw the elephants coming over the hill?
Here come the elephants.

What did Tarzan say when he saw the elephants coming over the hill with sunglasses on?
Nothing, he didn't recognise them.

You had to queue to see your favourite shows.

Movie food had two purposes. A large proportion of it was eaten but an equally large portion was used as some form of missile during the performance. The candy bar in the foyer provided basic supplies. In addition, a boy in uniform, usually with a peaked cap, hawked ice-creams and lollies inside the theatre. He carried his goods in a heavy tray attached to a leather strap over his shoulder. He advertised his goods in the same nasal tones used by paperboys.

Jaffas were essential. There'd be a really exciting bit in the movie and someone would throw one down the aisle. It rolled towards the front, with a "clunk" noise on each step on the wooden floor. Sometimes, there would be a whole lot and they'd sound like a stampede. Really scungy kids would pick them up and eat them later.

We used to get those rectangular ice-cream bars in square cones. The movie theatre was the only place you could get them.

My girlfriend and I always bought a packet of Fantales between us. We always ended up squabbling about who got Clark Gable.

I loved Fantales, but Mum banned them because they pulled the bands off my teeth.

I hated those kids who had lollies left to eat on the way home. Mine were gone with the first cartoon.

Let the Show Begin

Some theatres employed an organist to create atmosphere at the beginning of the performance. For matinee performances, this must have been a thankless task. In more up-market theatres, the organ would rise slowly, on a platform, from under the floor. The unfortunate organist was greeted with catcalls and pelted with Jaffas. To sustain a performance under these conditions required considerable fortitude.

Sometimes there would be such a riot that the theatre manager would come out. He'd threaten to close the show unless the noise stopped. It stopped for about two seconds.

I loved watching the curtains opening. At the Roxy there were enormous red tasselled curtains, with shimmery gold ones underneath. They'd start the movie while the gold ones were opening. I always thought you saw the picture *through* the gold curtains. I never realised it was being projected *onto* them.

A man at the side used to pull on the rope to get the curtains back. I never understood how one rope moved two curtains.

Tom and Jerry always came up first. There'd be hoots and catcalls and then everyone would settle down and laugh. It was a great cartoon.

You could get in the front eight rows for one and threepence. To see the screen, you were virtually lying parallel to the floor. Even then, it was a bit of a strain.

Once the front stalls were full, they'd put a rope across the aisle. As soon as the cartoons started, kids would start sneaking up under the rope. Ushers would be flashing torches at you. One aisle would break through while they were guarding the other aisle. It happened every Saturday. By the end of the performance, there was hardly anyone in the front stalls.

You got a straw and sucked up some of your ice-cream, then

MATINEE MOVIES

Adventures of Robin Hood
Battle in Rogue River
Burning Arrows
Davy Crockett — Indian Scout
Dawn at Socorro
Duel in the Jungle
Kangaroo Kid
The Kidnappers
The Living Desert
Long John Silver
Lost Treasure of the Amazon
The Old Texas Trail
Three Came Home
Treasure of the Amazon

*Where does the Lone Ranger
    take his rubbish?*
*To the dump, to the dump, to the
    dump, dump, dump.*

blew it out. You'd hear some girl go "Ooohh wah" further down the front.

The back stalls were for couples. They didn't come to the matinees so much, but in the night-time performances, it was a hotbed.

The dress circle was really classy. You could drop things on people, but you felt a bit out of it during the matinee.

My little brother loved the cartoons, but he started grizzling with the serials. By the end of the main feature he was unbearable. I always tried to lose him.

Cliffhangers

The cartoons at the beginning of the program provided the laughs, but it was the serials that brought the audiences back week after week. A climactic finish made it essential to know what happened next.

You left Tarzan swinging on a vine above a thousand foot drop. Of course you had to go back. Then, there'd be some poisonous snake about to drop on him, so you had to go back for another week.

The stagecoach would go over the cliff. Next week, they'd replay it at the beginning and some miracle would intervene to stop it being pulverised at the bottom of the ravine.

The Indian would fire his arrow and it'd be heading straight for the oblivious hero while the curtains were closing.

Spikes on a wall closing in on the hero. There'd be one just about to pierce his neck. Of course you went back.

Superman was the best because you knew he was fighting real evil. You always knew he was going to win, but somehow, you could never be quite sure.

I had a strong sense of identification with Tarzan. That's who I wanted to be. Him or Johnny Weissmuller. I used to think about swinging on the telegraph wires on the way home.

A genuine Australian western.

Batman and Robin was great because there was a kid in it. He was a bit of a twit, but it made you feel you could get somewhere in life.

We loved the westerns. There'd always be kids making comments — "Get him, get him, he's behind you." It felt that real.

There was a Robin Hood serial which was great. They got hold of some horses and it became very like a western towards the end.

Main Feature

The serial was followed by interval during which kids replenished their food and missiles. The beleaguered organist played on and Val Morgan advertisements flashed up on the screen. The commentary for these slide advertisements was given by the projectionist. The advertisements were for products as diverse as Roses Chocolates and the local record shop. In some theatres, an usher stood at the door of the theatre and rang a bell to

THE BIG MOVIES

Affair to Remember
Around the World in Eighty Days
Ben Hur
The Birds
Blackboard Jungle
Breakfast at Tiffany's
Bridge on the River Kwai
Cleopatra
55 Days at Peking
The Great Escape
The Greatest Story Ever Told
The Incredible Shrinking Man
It's a Mad, Mad, Mad, Mad World
Journey to the Centre of the Earth
My Fair Lady
The King and I
Oklahoma
On the Waterfront
Psycho
The Robe (first in cinemascope)
Twelve Angry Men
Seven Year Itch
Some Like it Hot
South Pacific
Spartacus
West Side Story

signify the end of interval. There was an immediate stampede back into the theatre, as the opening title of the main feature came up.

Sometimes a kid would have a birthday party. The manager would stand up on the stage with the cake and call the kid up to blow out the candles. Then we'd sing "Happy Birthday". Some smart alec would always louse it up.

I never understood why they put on a main feature. I thought the serials were much better.

The main feature was often more of the same. You could send your kid to the movies safe in the knowledge it was no sex, all violence.

The Disney features were the best. They were really fun, even ones like *Fantasia* which were supposed to be good for you too.

I loved Hayley Mills. I knew if I looked like that, life would have been perfect.

I saw all the Abbott and Costello movies. They all made me nearly sick with laughter.

At our local theatre the screen wasn't big enough for the film. At the end, you voted whether next week you'd have the top or bottom half. All the big kids who came with their girlfriends and just wanted to Kiss, voted for the bottom half.

There weren't many Australian pictures, but I remember *Jedda*. It made you realise that there was more to Central Australia than Ayer's Rock.

I loved *Bush Christmas*. I went to see it three weeks in a row.

Night-time Movies

Going to the matinee was a very different experience to a night-time visit to the movies. At night, with parents, the movies was a dress-up occasion. Sitting in the stalls lost its

WHAT THE THEATRES
WERE CALLED

Arcadia
Astor
Astoria
Astra
Capitol
Chelsea
Civic
Coronet
Embassy
Empire
Esquire
Grosvenor
Jewel
Kings
Majestic
Mayfair
Odeon
Orion
Palace
Paris
Plaza
Prince Edward
Regent
Rio
Ritz
Royal
Savoy
Southern Cross
State
Vogue
Windsor

attraction. Upstairs was considered preferable. Some families who were regular movie goers booked a block of family seats for a year.

Bush Christmas was a great Australian film.

Mum and Dad had a block of five seats. They had one of those love seats, without the arm rest. We thought that was a bit much for parents.

We went into town to see *The King and I*. Dad booked balcony seats. I was so excited, I couldn't pay any attention to the movie. I thought everyone was looking at us because we were sitting in a balcony.

At night-time there was the *Movietone News* before the feature. The guy who did the commentary had a really memorable voice. He must have done thousands.

There were special newsreels cinemas. The program went for an hour, but it was continuous and you could stay as long as you liked. They were always small, narrow theatres, really grotty.

I remember *South Pacific* going all different colours. Movies were magic and that was real magic.

We went to every movie with Doris Day in it. Mum thought they were fantastic, especially if Rock Hudson was in them too. I thought Doris Day was yuk.

Mum didn't really approve of films, especially American ones. But she came out of *Ben Hur* and declared it was a highly educational movie. Maybe she thought chariot racing was a healthy sport.

Time for Teenagers

American and in cinemascope — always popular.

From the mid-1950s, movies began to be made for the teenage market. James Dean, Elvis Presley and Gidget movies catered cleanly and simply, if not profoundly, for the passions of youth.

ROBERT NEWTON   *Long John* SILVER

KIT TAYLOR as "Jim Hawkins"

CONNIE GILCHRIST

CinemaScope   Print by TECHNICOLOR

A JOSEPH KAUFMAN Production

Released by Twentieth Century-Fox

General Exhibition

We thought *Jailhouse Rock* was incredibly wild. We didn't see *Rock around the Clock* until after it. Then we knew we'd found the real thing.

I wasn't allowed to see *Rebel without a Cause*. I went anyway and felt a bit disappointed. I thought I was going to be incited to rebellion.

I went to the *Gidget* movies with my girlfriends, hoping I'd meet some boy. Of course it was full of girls hoping to meet boys.

I was terribly revved up after I saw *The Wild One*. I wanted to be like Marlon Brando. But of course I went home and had my baked dinner like I always did.

Whatever the session, whatever the movie, the movies always ended the same way. People clapped and then as the first bars of 'God Save the Queen' played, the audience rose to its feet. As the flag fluttered, the Queen appeared on her horse. Clearly, she took the ceremony seriously, and so did the audience. No-one moved until the anthem was finished and the curtains were closed.

I am Shirley Temple,
The girl with the curly hair.
I've got two pretty dimples.
And I wear my hair down there.

CHAPTER SIXTEEN

Tune in Again Tomorrow

Jingle bells,
Robin smells,
Batman flew away.
Superman lost his undies,
Flying TAA.

Radio Time

If the Saturday flicks were the treat of the week for the baby boomers, radio was daily bread and butter. Radio had emerged from the wartime years in a very healthy state. The shortage of newsprint during the war and radio's powerful propaganda potential meant that it had become very important in most Australian families, both for news and entertainment.

The Serials

Serials took up a large slice of radio time. In the 1950s, more than 200 different episodes of serials were broadcast in Australia every day. Many of these were daytime serials which catered for housewives. Some were family shows, broadcast at breakfast or in the evening. But the 4 o'clock to 7 o'clock timeslot catered mainly for children and the serial was the favourite form.

In radio, as at the movies, the serial had a particular fascination for children. In many cases, the characters and stories were the same on radio and in movie serials. On radio, visual details were provided by a narrator or by an innocent bystander whom the scriptwriters slotted into the frenetic activity of the story for that particular purpose.

The serials were on between 6 and 7 o'clock. That suited us, because Mum insisted we get home by six. We all sat round the wireless listening to people being captured, crashing

We all loved listening to the radio.

aeroplanes, stopping stagecoaches and rescuing women. It was thrill a minute stuff.

Biggles' war lasted a lot longer than anyone else's. He was always out in the jungle with Algy, looking for someone who'd been shot down on a secret mission. The jungle was full of poisonous snakes, tigers and treacherous natives who'd pounce on anyone. It was always left hanging. Would Biggles get there in time?

I listened to *Hopalong Cassidy*, riding an imaginary horse backwards and forwards across the lounge room.

You got used to Australian actors doing upper-class British accents. The first time I heard a real British accent it sounded incredibly phoney.

You knew it was an Australian doing "Superman", but you never thought about it. Even when they changed the actor in the lead role you didn't worry. It was the story, what happened next, that was the important thing.

Even the serials based in Australia were a bit American. In *Return of the Golden Boomerang*, the Aborigines were like American Indians. They lived in tepees.

Smokey Dawson was Australian, but you felt he had a bit of go in him. He was like a real American cowboy. I got one of his records for my birthday. I played it till it wore out.

Serials were all about "goodies" and "baddies". Right triumphed over wrong. It was all very black and white. It would have never occurred to us that we were racist or prejudiced. After all, our side had won the war. We were very conscious of that.

Tarzan was a bit of a problem on radio because he couldn't say a lot besides, "Me — Tarzan. You — Jane." In spite of that, he managed to do a lot of screeching through the jungle and rescuing Jane. She was always getting herself in a terrible mess with savage lions or savage natives.

All the serials were for boys. At the time, I never thought about that. We listened, but we weren't passionate about them. The adventure format simply didn't include us. But at least Lois Lane had a career.

RADIO SERIALS

The Air Adventures of Biggles
Superman
The Crimson Trail
Return of the Golden Boomerang
Twilight Ranger
Hopalong Cassidy
Smokey Dawson
The Gang
The Adventures of Charlie Chan
Dick Tracy

Speed King
Tarzan
Hop Harrigan
Sea Hound

Children's Hour

Popular children's serials ran on the commercial stations. However, there was serious competition from the A.B.C's *Children's Hour* which began at 5.30 pm. It incorporated its own serial, the much loved *Muddle-headed Wombat*, serialised books, had a lively music segment and also the Argonaut's Club which children could join and contribute to. At its peak, the club had more than 150 000 members. The *Children's Hour* always began with the same song:

Old Mother Hubbard and Jack and Jill
And Tom the Piper's son;
Leave your cupboard, forget your spill —
And come and have some fun!
The wireless says to hurry and run
So leave your games and toys,
The wireless says the time has come
For all the girls and boys . . .
So, come with a hop, a skip and a run —
It's time for the session, it's time for the fun.

Each night, children did just what the wireless said, and sat entranced for an hour.

Mac, the presenter, was like a really nice Dad. Jimmie was a real clown, always doing silly things with his car and making mistakes. There was always a lot of laughing.

When I was little, I seemed to spend the whole day waiting for the *Muddle-headed Wombat*. Even when I was much older, I loved it.

I wrote in for my membership of Argonauts. I couldn't wait to find out my ship and my number. I was Diogenes 13. I never forgot it. It was like a code name.

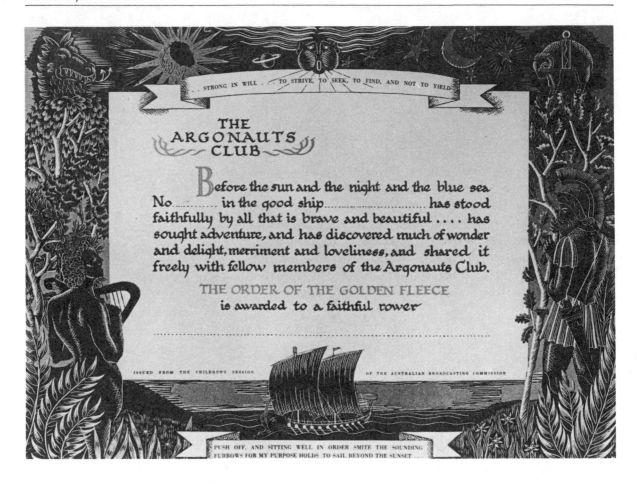

Winning certificates was an important part of being an Argonaut.

When you sent in a poem or a story, you'd be desperate, waiting and hoping it would be read out. My brother was always trying to switch over to the serials and I'd keep switching back to the A.B.C. I felt incredibly proud when they read out my poem. I won a blue certificate.

I used to send in a lot of paintings. Phidias, the art man, obviously couldn't read them out over the air, but he gave really good descriptions. "Socrates 4 has sent in a wonderful picture of four ducks — I particularly like that cloudy sky there — and the feed bucket right at the front." You'd be sitting there staring at the speaker, pictures rushing through your head.

There was a great session with Tom the naturalist. He explained about frogs in such a way that you had to rush out and get a jar of tadpoles.

A Family Affair

Radio also provided entertainment for the whole family. For certain programs, families would sit down and literally 'watch' the radio.

The dial was lit with a yellow light. All the stations for all the states were along six different bands. Then, up the top, on the short wave, there were Helsinki, Rome, Auckland and London. It seemed anything was possible.

We had an old bakelite radio. Then we got a Kreisler radiogram in two-tone pink and grey. It was the most modern thing I had ever seen.

The whole family used to listen to *Yes What?* waiting for Greenbottle to get caned. We'd roar with laughter and we'd always be quoting lines from the show. "Yes what?" Dad would say. "Yes sir!" we'd all chorus.

Life with Dexter was great. Mum was always saying, "You're as bad as Ashley and Janey." That was what the Dexters' kids were called.

Mum could do Eth from *Take it from Here* perfectly. If she wanted to jolt Dad out of a bad mood, she'd start on her Eth voice. It was better than the real thing.

There was a horror session on the A.B.C. on Sunday nights called *It Walks by Night*. I couldn't walk up the hall by myself afterwards.

I loved the radio plays. But I'd drive Mum mad by asking, "What does she look like?" We could tell all the actors by their voices, but you still wanted to know what they looked like.

I got *Blue Hills* by osmosis. We listened to it every night with tea. Even though I wasn't particularly interested, the characters became part of my life.

Our family were quiz show fanatics. We listened to Bob Dyer and Jack Davey. On *Pick-a-Box* half the family would be yelling "Take the box!" The rest of us would yell, "Take the money!"

Dad was the only one who could actually answer any of the questions.

There was a Palmolive *Secret Sound* contest, in which you had to identify the sound and send in your answer with six soap wrappers. I had three tries and sent in eighteen wrappers. I still didn't get the Morris Minor.

I was on Keith Smith's *Pied Piper Show*. I'd always, always wanted to be on it. I complained about my brother and how he teased me. I felt a bit ashamed when it came out.

Radio programs had something for everyone.

Baby boomer brains.

I loved the *Quiz Kids* with John Dease. I had a fantasy about being on a show and getting all the answers right. The only barrier was my ignorance.

Radio DJs and Teens

From the beginning of the 1950s, there was a tentative recognition of what was coyly termed the 'teen' market to cater for the older baby boomers. The American terms, 'hit parade' and 'disc jockey' slowly came into use. Hit parade shows with ordinary teenagers as guests were popular. Until the advent of rock and roll, these shows played the same easy-listening, popular music as adult music shows. For light relief there were gimic songs such as *My Old Man's a Dustman*, *Flying Purple People Eater* and *Does your Chewing Gum Lose its Flavour on the Bedpost Overnight?*.

When transistor radios came onto the market in the mid-1950s, it became impossible to ignore the trend towards rock and roll music. Imported rock and roll artists attracted enormous live audiences. Local artists such as Johnny O'Keefe were launching a home-grown industry. From 1956, television provided the news, drama, quiz shows and serials. Baby boomers born in the mid-1950s, never enjoyed the radio serials and dramas of those a few years older. Increasingly, radio, except for the A.B.C., played music and not much else. A large part of that music catered for teenagers, with the 'crazy man' DJ's such as Bob Rogers, Tony Withers, John Laws and Ward Pally Austin.

You could go and sit in your room with your radio and be in a different world. Bill Haley, Little Richard, Elvis, Buddy Holly and all the rest.

I loved all the teenage death songs, *Tell Laura I Love Her*, *Teen Angel*, *Leader of the Pack*. My girlfriend and I used to cry over them. God knows what was going on in our heads.

There was real rock and roll. Then there was the really soppy stuff — the Paul and Paula, Bobby Rydell, Fabian, Brook Benton. I loved it all.

Mum told me she didn't want me to be one of those teenagers. But she gave me a transistor for Christmas. It weighed a ton, but I could actually take it to the beach. Mum told me I'd better not get any ideas.

TOP 40 MEMORIES

Shout — Johnny O'Keefe
Walk Like a Man — Four Seasons
Bye Bye Baby — Col Joye
Tutti Frutti — Little Richard
That'll be the Day — Buddy Holly
Maybelline — Chuck Berry
Corrine, Corrine — Jerry Lee Lewis
Diana — Paul Anka
Sheila — Tommy Roe
Rave On — Buddy Holly
Donna — Ritchie Valens
Run to Him — Bobby Vee

Hats off to Larry — Del Shannon
Chantilly Lace — Big Boppa
It's my Party — Lesley Gore
Save the Last Dance for Me — the Drifters
Let's Twist Again — Chubby Checker
Flying Purple People Eater — Sheb Woolley
Swinging School — Bobby Rydell
Running Bear — Johnny Preston
Mr Custer — Larry Verne
Personality — Lloyd Price
Yes Sir, that's my Baby — Ricky Nelson
Crying — Johnny Ray
I'm Sorry — Brenda Lee
Rebel Rouser — Duane Eddy
Love Letters in the Sand — Pat Boone
Twenty Miles is a Long Long Way — Ray Brown and the
   Whispers
Boom, Boom Baby — Crash Craddock
Pub with No Beer — Slim Dusty
Rock Around the Clock — Bill Haley
I Remember You — Frank Ifield
Shake, Rattle and Roll — Johnny Devlin
All I have to do is Dream — Everly Brothers
Yakety Yak — the Coasters
The Great Pretender — the Platters
Stagger Lee — Lloyd Price
See You Later Alligator — Bill Haley
Limbo Rock — Chubby Checker

TV Takes Over

It wasn't only the advent of the rock and roll market that destroyed the radio format of the 1940s and 1950s. The coming of television in 1956 eventually destroyed both the Saturday afternoon picture show and radio. Television virtually took over radio and added pictures. *Pick-a-Box*, the *Quiz Kids*, the serials, drama, news and sport had the same basic form as radio. 'Radio with pictures' was how most of the baby boomers regarded television. Those baby boomers born in the television era missed the experiences of radio serials and Saturday afternoon flicks. Television became a total entertainment.

Daniel Boone was one of many westerns.

The first time I saw TV I was terribly disappointed. There was Brian Henderson reading the news when it was time for *Superman*. I thought TV would have exactly the same programs as radio, but there would be pictures as well.

We'd go and watch TV in H. G. Palmer's window on the way home from school. We'd stand there, banked four or five deep, just staring at the box, not even able to hear it.

I was shameless. I was best friends with anyone, just anyone, who owned a TV.

You could get your photo taken at Luna Park behind a TV screen. I took it to school. Everybody was really impressed until someone saw my dress poking out underneath.

I found it very disappointing there were only three stations. I thought it would be like radio.

My father swore we'd never get a TV. Mum talked him into

renting one for school holidays. He said it was useful for the news, but it was the *Phil Silvers Show* that really got him in.

Our family spent two years transfixed by the box. We watched everything and anything. By the time we switched it off, we'd all grown up.

A 21 inch set was a real status symbol. My Dad went one better and got remote control. "Changes the channel right across the room with AUTOMATION."

Favourite Television Shows

'Seven is heaven, two will do, nine is fine.' Dial switching had little effect in television-land. The same basic fare appeared on all the channels. Only the A.B.C. was rather more intellectual and highbrow. Children responded by watching it less, preferring imported American shows on the commercials.

I don't know one boy who wasn't painfully in love with Annette Funicello from the Mouseketeers.

I loved Cubby. I had a picture of him, in ears, inside my wardrobe door. I thought that was a very cool thing to do.

Sometimes we'd sing the Mouseketeers song at lunchtime at school. One of the teachers would swoop on us before we got past M I C ... K E Y, and tell us to stop that American nonsense.

My aunt sent me pair of Mickey Mouse ears from America. I was amazed that they were plastic. I'd always thought they'd have to be wood or something.

Before we got TV, we went down the street in our dressing-gowns every Sunday night to watch *Disneyland* at a neighbour's place. We weren't allowed to go unless our rooms were clean.

We loved the comedies — *I Love Lucy*, *Sergeant Bilko*, *The Honeymooners*, even *The Three Stooges*. Some of them, like *Leave it to Beaver* and *The Nelsons* were a bit too cute.

'Come on everybody it' s six o'clock.'

I was a western fanatic. I watched *The Lone Ranger, Wells Fargo, Kit Carson, Wyatt Earp, Maverick, Have Gun Will Travel, Gene Autry, Rawhide, Bonanza, Wagon Train, Annie Oakley, Cheyenne, Daniel Boone* and *Texas Rangers* plus all the movies. It took up most of my childhood.

I really believed Mr Ed could talk. In fact, I believed anything I saw on TV. I was gullible.

The *Twilight Zone* scared me so much that I had to watch it. Knowing it was on and not watching it was worse.

Sea Hunt was my favourite serial. The only problem was that you couldn't play it.

There were all these smart animals on TV — Lassie, Rin Tin Tin, Mr Ed. I got very disillusioned with my dog Rover.

I got totally hooked on *Dr Kildare*. Next to him, *Ben Casey* was nothing.

Television was just so American, that when you saw something Australian like *Homicide* it took you a while to adjust to it.

They put wrestling on TV and my mother watched it. I couldn't believe that my mother could watch anything like that.

There was a roller-skating show called *The Roller Game*. The girls were really rough and punched each other up. We weren't allowed to watch it, but we did.

I watched *Peyton Place* and realised you weren't supposed to kiss with your mouth closed. It helped me grow up.

Six O'Clock Rock with Johnny O'Keefe was my favourite show. I was an only child and I wasn't allowed out. It gave me hope that life would be fun when I was.

The Samurai
National Velvet
Zorro
The Munsters
Red Skelton Hour
Fugitive
Space Station
Wild Kingdom
The Addams Family
Bewitched
My Three Sons
Z Cars
Astroboy
Beverley Hillbillies
The Jetsons

CHAPTER SEVENTEEN

A Good Read

I pity the crow, I pity the rook,
I pity the kid who swipes my book.

Young Readers

Australians are prodigious readers, a fact that does not fit easily with our rugged, outdoor image of ourselves. In the 1950s, before the advent of television, reading was even more important as entertainment. Australians read widely and from an early age. Some reading material was imposed on children and was not particularly welcome. Other material was the children's own choice, but not approved of by adults. In general, the range of books available was very much narrower than today's.

Reading was all-absorbing.

We had one book of nursery rhymes, handed down through five children. I was number five. It was pretty tattered by the time I got it.

We had a book about the three little kittens who washed their mittens. The kittens all had nice dresses and an old style clothes line. I can still see it.

Every night my mother read us *The Three Bears*. It never occurred to us that we should have something different.

"Pooh Bear" and "Peter Rabbit" were favourite characters. Very English, but then everything was.

I thought "Milly Molly Mandy" was a real name. I wished my mother had called me that.

I loved the Golden Books. The cover came off the *Saggy Baggy Elephant* and my world was destroyed.

We used to have *Little Black Sambo* read to us. We didn't know what racist was.

From hearing stories at mother's knee, children became readers themselves, a process filled with promise, not always immediately fulfilled.

I learnt to read quickly, but I couldn't see the point. All the stories about "Wendy can jump. Can Wendy jump? Wendy jumps." seemed totally boring. I thought my mother reading to me was much better.

I learnt to read before I went to school. The teacher was really angry about it. I had to read the same primers as the rest of the class.

Learning to read was okay, but I really wanted to be able to read a newspaper, like Dad.

Limited Choice

In the post-war era, far less was published in paperback than is published today. Children's books were usually hardback and therefore expensive. A 'good book' was a substantial birthday present. There were fewer libraries and they were less accessible.

Our school library was a cupboard. You were only allowed one book a week, but you still got through the whole library in one year.

We had library lessons. They had nothing to do with books and everything to do with being quiet.

I went to the local library with Mum and marvelled at the number of books. There must have been a couple of hundred.

The mobile library was fantastic. Basically, it was just a truckload of books, but it was like stepping into another world.

GIRLS' BOOKS

Anne of Green Gables — L. M. Montgomery
Little Women — L. M. Alcott
Heidi — J. Spyri
Milly Molly Mandy — J. L. Brisley
The Secret Garden — Francis Hodgson Burnett
What Katy Did — Susan Coolidge

BOYS' BOOKS

Biggles — W. E. Johns
Swallows and Amazons — Arthur Ransome
Just William books — R. Crompton
The Jungle Book — Rudyard Kipling
Robinson Crusoe — Daniel Defoe
Treasure Island — R. L. Stevenson

ANYONE COULD READ THESE

Doctor Dolittle — Hugh Lofting
The Secret Seven — Enid Blyton
The Famous Five — Enid Blyton
The Borrowers — Mary Norton
The Bobbsey Twins — Laura L. Hope
Five Children and It — E. Nesbit
The Wind in the Willows — K. Grahame
Black Beauty — A. Sewell
My Friend Flicka — Mary O'Hara
Lassie — Eric Knight
Peter Pan — J. M. Barrie
The Water Babies — Charles Kingsley
The Swiss Family Robinson — J. Wyss

Boys and Girls

Because books were a relatively valuable commodity, children all read the same books. Reading preferences, like most other activities, tended to be divided by sex.

I desperately wanted to read *Biggles* because I saw my brothers playing it. But our library was divided in shelves, "girls", "boys" and "general". Naturally, *Biggles* was in the "boys" section. Finally, I got hold of a copy. It was full of planes and fighting and very boring.

The first proper book I read was the *Magic Faraway Tree*. I read all the *Secret Seven* and then all the *Famous Five* series. I loved them. It was vital to know who the characters were so you could be part of lunchtime conversation.

A lot of books went in series. I remember looking at all the titles on the back of the *Famous Five* and thinking "I'm nearly there, I'm nearly there".

I thought Noddy and Big Ears were really stupid. I was relieved when I liked the *Secret Seven*. I felt normal again.

Getting through the *Anne of Green Gables* series was quite an achievement. None of them were as good as the first. You always wanted to go back to Anne at the orphanage and her arrival at Green Gables.

I read about Sophy the seal being thrown back into the sea by Dr Dolittle. I knew I had to be a vet.

I read all the *What Katy Did* books. I felt betrayed when she became so saintly.

The Jungle Book was really important to me. I desperately wanted to be Mowgli. The one thing I couldn't work out was where he got his underpants.

When I read *Heidi* I wanted a Swiss blouse. I could just see myself herding goats after school.

I read everything I could about horses. *Black Beauty*, *My Friend Flicka* and *National Velvet* were the only ones that stuck in my head.

Famous Five on yet another adventure.

After I read the *Princess and Curdie*, I pestered my mother to have stars painted on my ceiling.

I believed in *Borrowers*. I knew there were little people under the floor. They seemed really clever to me because they ignored the bits and pieces I put out specially for them.

Our teacher was always trying to steer us towards "good books". Finally, she forced me to read *The Lion the Witch and the Wardobe*. She must have been pleased. I read all the C. S. Lewis books.

I loved the E. Nesbit books. After reading *Five Children and It*, I excavated my brother's sandpit.

Lassie made me cry so much, that I had to read it in private.

The classics didn't always appeal.

Robinson Crusoe   TOWNSEND

The story is about a man who is shipwrecked on an island and ~~too~~ lived there for thirty odd years with a cannibal he found. The story is by Daniel Defoe.

I think the story could be ~~true~~, but to people with good imagination it would be an interesting ~~book~~. I don't think Friday would have learned English so quickly as he did, and Crusoe couldn't make so many instruments as he did In some parts it was a bit dull and in other parts it was alright If he had lived there thirty years he would have run out of powder and shot.

On the whole I don't think it was a very interesting book but some people may like it.

Classics

Most of the classics read by Australian children were English books. They were often seen by teachers and librarians as intrinsically superior to the Australian product. Through Charles Kingsley's *The Water Babies*, Australian children were swept into the mythology of chimney sweeps. *Alice in Wonderland* gave a somewhat heretical view of royalty. *Peter Pan* cemented the tradition of nannies firmly into the Australian imagination (although not into Australian life). *The Secret Garden* reinforced the powerfully misleading seasonal perceptions created by hot Christmas dinners and poems about autumn leaves. Despite more exotic settings, even *Swallows and Amazons* and *Robinson Crusoe* were unmistakably English. However, some Australian books played an important part in the Australian childhood.

They too, perpetuated their own myths by emphasising the rural aspects of Australian life.

Seven Little Australians was about the sort of Australian kids we felt we were. And it was so sad. Even the boys cried when Judy died.

The Children of the Dark People by Frank Dalby Davison had a big impression on me. I used to wonder what it would have been like to be an Aborigine, the sort of things you'd think about. And of course, anyone brought up in the 1950s was worried about not wearing clothes.

Every time I went the short cut to school, I used to hope I'd meet a kangaroo and get lost. Even in suburbia, *Dot and the Kangaroo* had its effect.

GOLDEN OLDIES — THE WELL-LOVED GOLDEN BOOKS

The Saggy Baggy Elephant
The Poky Little Puppy
Frosty the Snowman
Jack and the Beanstalk
Little Red Riding Hood
Scuffy the Tugboat
The Little Yellow Taxi
Tootle
Old MacDonald Had a Farm
The Three Little Pigs
The Three Bears

Dot and the Kangaroo — an Australian favourite.

Even when I was too old for it, I used to read *Blinky Bill*. I still find koalas in overalls really appealing.

Snugglepot and Cuddlepie was so good that I still think of banksias as evil plants.

Our teacher read *The Magic Pudding* out loud. He got very embarrassed by some of what he regarded as the "coarse bits". At the end, he said it should have been better written.

I read all the *Billabong* series of Mary Grant Bruce. You felt good being Australian.

Regular Reading

At school, children were encouraged to read, if only the dreary school magazine. This was issued regularly each month, in uniform grey. But at home, there were parents who found an obsession with books disturbing. Others happily shared the obsession.

"You'll ruin your eyes." Mum was convinced I read far too much. She thought it was bad for me and unnatural.

We had to be in bed by 7.30 p.m. It used to infuriate me. I'd nick Dad's torch and read under the covers. I got hell when I was caught.

Dad used to read to us every night. I was amazed when I found out that not every family did it.

We'd all be reading over the breakfast table. It used to drive Mum wild. She'd worry about us eating boiled eggs and catching buses, and we'd be in faraway land.

Mum would look for something "useful" to do if she caught us reading. We had a tree down the paddock so the four of us would retreat up there and read for hours.

Light Reading

As well as books, comics and other light reading, played a

vital part in children's lives. Comics, annuals, girls' romances and 'Boys' Own' books usually came out of weekly pocket money.

I'd get one shilling and threepence lunch money and go without lunch to buy books from the "Girls' Own" library They were full of stories about the head girl and how somebody unfairly elbowed their way into the lacrosse team. I never found out what lacrosse was.

I loved the *Boys' Annual*. My uncle gave it to me every Christmas. It took me until I was fifteen to realise all the stories were basically the same.

The "Boys' Own" stories were my favourites. British fighter pilots were the goodies. Japanese and Germans were the baddies. Sometimes an English man would look bad. Usually, he'd turn up trumps in the end. When they were lying crashed in the jungle, there'd always be a rattlesnake or a man-eating tiger around.

A lot of American comics came out of the Korean war. They were a lot zappier than the English stuff. The pictures of people getting killed were much more graphic. There was a lot of "Zap!" and "Kapow!" exclamations. You'd sit there, going "Zap! Pow!" You could always tell when someone was reading one.

Illustrated classics were an upmarket comic. *The Hunchback of Notre Dame* was terrific. *Treasure Island* actually became readable and *Mutiny on the Bounty* was great. Even teachers didn't mind you reading them because they thought it might lead you onto "good" literature.

The *Phantom* was the best comic. It was really exciting and you could turn it into a game. You could get things like Phantom rings, which made it even better.

I loved the Disney comics — *Mickey Mouse* and *Donald Duck*. Mum thought they were disgusting. But I bought one every week and swapped them too.

I remember the *Archie and Veronica* comics. You could get them in a bound volume, smaller but thicker than a normal comic book. It still only took about an hour to read.

FAVOURITE COMICS

Phantom
Superman
Archie and Veronica
Casper The Friendly Ghost
Donald Duck
Mickey Mouse
The Lone Ranger
Mandrake
Nancy
Flying Doctor
Prince Valiant

What kind of cat is found in a library?
A CATalogue.

My cousin and I bought *Mad* magazine together. We'd actually get sick with laughter.

We'd wait for my father to come home with the evening paper — first the comics and then the murders.

I got hooked on *Brenda Starr* and her mystery man. I've always wanted a black orchid.

L'il Abner seemed really serious to me. I couldn't understand why my grandfather thought it was funny.

Books - ideal gifts for adults and children

102G1: "Twilight on the Floods," by Marguerite Steen, deals with the Ashanti war and 19th century England. A remarkable novel. Post. 1/-. **15/-**

102G2: "Lena Geyer," by Marcia Davenport, is a fictitious biography which skilfully portrays a great singer and a lovable woman. Post. 9d. **12/6**

102G3: "Arabella," by Georgette Heyer, is a witty period novel with a romantic flavour. Postage 6d. At **10/6**

102G4: "Dinner at Antoine's," by Francis Parkinson Keyes, transports the happy reader to romance and tragedy in Louisiana. Post. 1/-. **15/-**

102G5: "Daddy Long Legs," Jean Webster's evergreen favourite, is a whimsical, happy tale. Post. 4½d. **5/3**

102G6: "Seven Little Australians," by Ethel Turner. The classic beloved by Australians of all ages. Price **9/6** Postage 6d.

102G7: "A Little Bush Maid," by Mary Grant Bruce. The first famous "Billabong" story. Post. 6d. At **9/6**

102G8: "Biggles, Air Commodore," by W. E. Johns, is another thrilling tale of adventure. Postage 6d. At **6/6**

102G9: "Connie Christie Annual" in the latest edition is delightfully illustrated in colour. Fairy stories and verse. Postage 7½d. Priced at **5/11**

102G10: "Margaret Tarrant Story Book" has 128 pages of selected fairy, adventure and animal stories and 8 lovely colour plates. Post. 1/-. **12/3**

102G11: "Favourite Book for Children" (also editions specially for Boys, Girls or Toddles). Stories selected to suit each age. Beautiful colour plates, line drawings. Postage 7½d. Price **3/11**

102G12: "Tuck's Annual" will delight boys and girls with its pictures, tales, hobbies, history, travel, verse, games and puzzles. Post. 10½d. **12/6**

26   DAVID JONES', BOX 503 G.P.O., SYDNEY.   CARRIAGE EXTRA

The *Sunday Telegraph* brought out the *Junior Telegraph* in 1954. It had sports and serials and comics and jokes and *Ripley's 'Believe it or Not'*. Bliss!

We used to fight over the kid's section in the Sunday papers. A couple of times it got so heated the paper actually got ripped to pieces.

Prince Valiant was the first thing I turned to every Sunday . . . still do.

"Doing" Books

Heavier reading became obligatory in high school, when children were required to 'do' a novel each year. This meant reading it at least once, doing character analyses, commenting on passages, knowing the plot and pulling it to bits. The range of books dissected in this way was remarkably narrow.

Everybody did *Wind in the Willows* in first year high. It was the first and last book I read in five years.

We went over and over *Pride and Prejudice*. I managed to forget the entire novel from the moment I'd finished the English paper for the Leaving Certificate.

We did the *Forsythe Saga* novels by Galsworthy. I really enjoyed reading them, but I had no idea what I was supposed to say about them.

Our teacher decided we should learn whole passages out of *A Tale of Two Cities*. I had a good memory, so I did well. She never knew I hadn't actually read the book.

We had to do the Brontes, Jane Austen and Robert Louis Stevenson. We were interested in hairdos and boys. It didn't connect.

I was quite surprised when I read Dickens after I left school. I discovered he was a really good writer.

Silence in the court.
The monkey wants to talk.
The first one to talk is the monkey.

Extra Good Reads

Other books reflecting more closely the interests of the average teenager, were hard to find. It was a time when *Tropic of Capricorn*, *Playboy* and anything else which could corrupt the morals of youth, was banned. But there were lucky finds.

I nearly cried when I read *Catcher in the Rye*. It was such a relief that someone felt like I did.

I got hold of *Sunlovers* magazine. It was promoted as a "health" magazine, for nudists. It had pictures of tits. To my friends, I was a prince.

I found *Function of the Orgasm* by Wilhelm Reich in a second-hand shop. I was overawed. I knew even my mother wouldn't have known all that stuff.

There was so much public fuss over *Lady Chatterley's Lover* that it was essential reading in our neighbourhood. All the kids got copies. But it was far too literary for what we wanted.

My older brother used to hide *Man* magazines under his mattress. He didn't have a girlfriend but he was so obsessed by sex that he read them constantly. Finally, he got a girl, then I spent all day reading them.

CHAPTER EIGHTEEN

If You Can't Be Good, Be Careful

I love you, I love you,
I love you almighty.
I wish your pyjamas,
Were next to my nightie.
Now don't be mistaken,
Don't be misled.
I mean on the clothesline,
Not in the bed.

The Facts of Life

For the baby boomer, the transition to adulthood was not a smooth or easy one. Lack of information and misinformation made the process far more difficult and painful than it needed to be. The change in sexual mores that occurred in the late 1960s was probably, in part, a reaction, against the sexual secrecy and evasiveness the baby boomers grew up with. SEX was not a word that was used much in the 1950s, especially in polite company. For children, little information was available on this vital topic.

Baby boomers accumulated sexual knowledge wherever they could. Snippets gleaned from the evening newspapers made it clear sex was something to do with divorce and rape. Doris Day movies associated it coyly with courtship. It was obvious that people such as parents would have no sensible information on the subject. Double beds seemed more like a space-saving device than cradles of passion. In a natural quest for information, children either drew their own conclusions or sought information from other children.

I found a condom on the beach and innocently put it in my shell collection. My parents were too embarrassed to enlighten me.

> Dear Stephen,
>   I have brought some chocolate crackles to school and, as a token of our sincere love for each other I will give you one. Please do not refuse it, as it would break my heart into a million fragments of grief.
>
>   Your ever-loving
>   girlfriend,
>   Mal.

The course of true love never runs smooth.

My mother used to explain to me that children grew inside their mothers. She made a big deal of it, as if I was ignorant of the fact. I wanted to know HOW, but that was privileged information.

From the number of pregnant woman walking round it was pretty obvious that the stork theory was nonsense.

You could gauge fairly well what your parents would or wouldn't tell you. I guessed mine wouldn't tell me anything. I was right.

My mother was always telling me to leave my little sister alone. It was no use telling her my little sister wouldn't leave me alone. Mum thought boys were awful and girls were pure.

Our neighbourhood was self educated in matters of sex. The bamboo patch was the accepted place. We knew instinctively that it was something you kept from parents.

Sex Education

Children made early and continuing efforts at educating themselves in matters of sex. In spite of community prudishness and a general public disinclination to admit that sex actually occurred, some organisations actually advocated and promoted sex education. Inevitably, such organisations shared the general coyness and embarrassment occasioned by any mention of bodily contact. In an attempt to make sex education mature, scientific and value packed, the information itself was often obscured.

The male also has a part to play in the reproduction of life.

As Mum and I drove home from the Mothers and Daughters night, she said hurriedly, "I'm pleased that's all cleared up now," and revved the car loudly.

My friend wasn't allowed to play with me for a week after I went to the sex education week. Her mother thought she'd get contaminated.

The night they had the talk for mothers and daughters, all the boys came down to the school and raced round outside screaming and whooping. That was the most exciting bit.

Making baby boomers.

Sex education was strictly segregated. Girls and mothers had sessions, which concentrated on topics such as 'The Wonder of a Woman's Body' and 'The Miracle Within'. The sessions for fathers and sons were equally obscure.

Without actually mentioning the term masturbation, they managed to imply that we'd all end up in the mad house if we kept at it.

We moved in very quick succession from "self abuse" to the horrors of V.D. It was pretty clear to me the direction I was heading in. It frightened me, but not enough to actually stop.

There were some awfully odd ideas. The priest told us if we respected our mothers we wouldn't masturbate. It sounded obscene.

They told us not to take any notice of old fashioned ideas. It really was quite all right to wash your hair while you were menstruating. Unfortunately, they didn't explain what menstruation was.

At the end of the lecture they showed a slide of the white cabbage moth, full frontal. It wasn't much use to someone who wanted to know about girls.

Sex education was·like the exemption clauses in an insurance contract.

I used to look at the V.D. warnings in the railway station toilets. I certainly didn't want to catch it and go blind and insane. It said "Chastity guarantees safety". I didn't know what chastity was.

Unmentionables

For most children, sex education was too obscure to prove useful in coping with the onslaught of puberty. In some cases, peers provided the necessary information, but in many cases, children found out what they needed to know on their own.

I realised that my under arms smelt and I was horrified. I kept having showers and sniffing at them to see if I could still smell it. It took me ages to realise that it was normal.

My first period was horrendous. My mother said "Don't stain the sheets," and gave me a box of Kotex and a belt. I had absolutely no idea what to do with it.

Everybody was getting breasts. Of course nobody ever put it like that. They just let you know they were wearing a bra. I finally persuaded my mother to buy me one with bits of sponge rubber in it. A sad sight.

Trainer bras they were called. I don't know who or what they trained.

We'd been told that "nocturnal emissions were completely normal". I had no idea what that meant. It was my mates who enlightened me.

I sent away for an information booklet from a packet of pads. I was too scared to ask my mother if it ever came.

I can remember trying to use my first tampon. I locked myself in the bathroom. Hopeless! The diagram didn't have anything that corresponded to me.

If all the boys lived over the sea,
What a good swimmer Sally
would be.

(from *The Guide to Virile Manhood*, P.J.L. Kenny, Seventh Edition):
Up till recent years V.D. was regarded as one of the greatest killers of mankind. Through its amazing progress medical science can cure venereal disease today if treatment is sought early and carried out by a fully qualified doctor. If sexual intercourse outside of marriage were to cease, these widespread and dangerous diseases would virtually disappear.

It is possible that there may be certain physical causes in regard to a lad being faced with the problem of masturbation. Clothing that is worn too tight may tend to cause irritation around the sex areas.

The physical effects of masturbation moderately practised may not be very marked. Nevertheless, the wise young man will be anxious to leave behind him this practice, which only too soon can become an iron-chain of habit. It is a selfish practice because it turn s a lad's thoughts and attention in on to himself and he becomes concerned with only the relief of his own sex urge and in bringing satisfaction to himself.

To become fit and keep fit, it is absolutely essential that you observe the following rules closely: (1) Exercise and play wisely. (2) Eat wholesome food. (3) Get sufficient sleep (nine to ten hours). (4) Get all the fresh air possible. (5) Keep clean.

(from *A Guide to Womanhood*):
Girls who expect to do well in school and in recreational activities, and ultimately to accomplish good and useful work in the world, cannot permit themselves to yield to every mood of self-indulgence. Nor can they let themselves develop a habit of retreating from the outside world into useless daydreaming and sexual reveries. The mind and body must be kept under reasonable discipline and directed into sound activities.

You may become conscious of the strong pulse of sex within your personality. In our society marriage and the fulfilment of this sex urge must wait until you are several years older, because your man will not be able to support you until he has been working at his job for a few years.

Boyfriends and Girlfriends

Encounters with the opposite sex were often horribly difficult. Peer pressure came into play. Having a girlfriend or boyfriend became the all important criterion of social success. Boys were called upon to perform, girls to resist.

I desperately wanted a girlfriend, but I had no idea how you got one. Finally, I asked a girl if she'd be my girlfriend. No one was more stunned than me when she said yes. I thought that was it. I was even more stunned when I found out there was more to it.

My sister got breasts, high heels and a boyfriend all in one year. I despised her because she couldn't run down hills anymore. I vowed it would never happen to me.

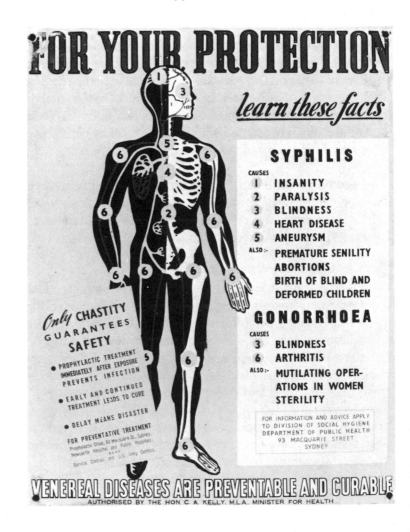

You'd have a girlfriend one day and you'd come to school the next day and she'd be giggling with her girlfriends. You'd hear on the grapevine that you'd been dropped. It was just one of those things girls did.

Being the one who never had a boyfriend was incredibly painful. Missing out at the age of twelve, you became the girl who always missed out. I pretended it didn't matter, but it was horrendous.

Everyone had a partner for the end of year school dance, but there were more boys than girls. I missed out. I felt there was something terribly wrong with me.

The first date — a tense experience.

The School Dance

The school dance was a ritual at which social failure could be witnessed in a profound and very public fashion. Some schools had the 'sixth class social' which supposedly launched children in a sensible and tidy fashion into sociable relationships with the opposite sex. Other schools waited until girls were fifteen, when they 'came out'. The white dress was de rigueur for girls. Boys were press-ganged into suits to act as their partners. Again, many found the ritual incredibly painful.

My mother chose the girl I took to the end of term school dance. I sat with her all night. I didn't dance. I didn't speak. When I got home, I just lay on my bed and sobbed.

The boy who took me to the dance got in the door and immediately took off with some other girl. He told me his mother made him invite me. I renounced boys, love and marriage forever.

All the boys stood up one end and all the girls were down the other. When it came time to dance, the boys would saunter down and pick off the girls one by one. The last couple was always the tallest girl and the shortest boy.

The fast crowd was outside the school hall. You could hear them laughing in the dark and see the light of cigarettes. The

The boys and the girls

fathers were supposed to be vigilantes for the night, but they didn't care as long as their own kids were inside.

The night of the school dance we got drunk and climbed up on the school roof. If felt like some vast sexual exploit.

Together at Last

Actual physical contact with the opposite sex followed a time of speculation and worry. Holding hands and the first kiss were momentous and difficult events.

On my first date we went to the pictures. There was an air of horrible tension between us. About half way through the movie I could sense his hand moving along the arm of the seat. Then he grabbed my hand. We both relaxed.

I was kissing this girl and suddenly, she began kissing with her tongue. I was horribly shocked. She told me it was French kissing. It began to seem okay.

Holding hands was the first step. Of course the ultimate was to be *seen* holding hands by your friends.

I was really scared of kissing the girl I was going out with. I was scared I'd be swept away on a tide of passion and be totally unable to control myself. Finally, she got so sick of waiting that she kissed me.

The Double Standard

Australian girls of the 1950s and 1960s were subject to the rigid morality of 'nice girls don't'. However, many boys, while subscribing to the same standard for girls, had no such scruples relating to themselves. The result of this double standard was widespread confusion, pretence and deceit.

We used to gossip about girls who "went too far". A lot of it was just malicious chatter about girls who were popular.

You'd be scared that if you went too far he'd think you were cheap. But if you didn't, he'd think you were frigid and drop you.

Nobody ever talked about what they actually did. It was all double talk. Upstairs inside, downstairs outside — all euphemisms.

It was supposed to be like a battle between the boy and the girl. You were always trying to stop them, they were always trying to make you. The theory ignored the fact that girls had sexual desire.

When you are married,
When you have twins,
Come to me for safety pins.

There was the numbers system girls used to talk about. One to ten. Ten was intercourse. Nobody ever admitted to that. An eight or a nine was very daring.

You'd boast to your mates how far you'd got with a girl. We all lied like mad.

Precautions

The question of contraception was a difficult one. Girls didn't think about it. If they had sex, it was supposed to be on a momentary impulse of being 'swept away'. It was up to the boy to take precautions.

I remember going to chemist shop after chemist shop. In every one there was a girl serving. You couldn't possibly ask a girl for Wetchex. I came away with a collection of Band-Aids and cotton tips.

If you went to the local chemist to get condoms, you were likely to get a lecture on morality. But you'd get them eventually, because the chemist was a mean old bastard who couldn't bear to miss out on a sale.

Any kid who managed to get condoms was a real Romeo. Never mind whether he had a girl or not.

Dressing with Style

From the late 1950s, with the advent of rock and roll, a definite teenage style of dressing developed. There was more than a simple transition from short pants to long pants, from shoes and socks to stockings and suspenders. Teenage clothes developed an identity of their own, deliberately provocative and outrageous, clearly delineated from the clothes of both adults and children.

I had three-tone ripple sole shoes. "They walk for you" the ads said. It was true. You felt almost disembodied.

I had tight peg trousers with a thin belt. They were in what was known as Mitchell blue with a gold thread. I wore them with a purple drape coat. I don't know if it impressed anybody else, but it certainly impressed me.

I had 14 inch cuffs on a pair of peg top green slacks. I wore them with crepe soled shoes known as "brothel creepers".

My father called desert boots "co-respondent shoes". I knew he disapproved, but I had no idea what he meant.

Drip dry shirts came in. You washed them in the shower and then left them to dry. They were woven plastic.

I thought the girls would go mad over me when I bought a Kookie jacket as in "77 Sunset Strip". No-one even noticed it.

If you couldn't afford a Kookie jacket, you got a Canadian lumber jacket.

There was a craze for Crash Craddock jumpers. It lasted about as long as Crash Craddock which wasn't very long.

Girls wore their cardigans back to front, buttoned down the back. It came from a "Gidget" movie.

If you were going to a dance, you wore a rope petticoat because that really spun out well. Sometimes, you wore a tulle petticoat under it, so your skirt would stick out all the time.

There was a craze for white frilly blouses with lace and milkmaid sleeves. And horrible tartan jerkins to wear over them.

You had to have the right figure. Big bust, tiny waist and be short and cute. Anyone else in a full skirt and a rope petticoat with a tight jumper looked ridiculous.

There were two girls on *Six O'Clock Rock* called Mandy and Candy. Real girls looked like them.

Crowning Glory

If clothes were important, so were hair styles. There were an enormous variety of hair creams for men, all of which promised to endow the wearer with a hairstyle which would capture the heart of the opposite sex.

I'd get home from school, rush into the bedroom, squeeze my pimples and then spend about three hours doing my hair.

Julie for now, Julie for ever,
Clarke for now, but not forever.

There was stuff called "Californian Poppy". It was like sump oil, but very effective.

You'd get the bit hanging down over your forehead. Everything would be slicked down to the duck's tail at the back. It looked like a major oil spill.

Dad would take one look at my hair and yell, "You're not going out like that!" Mum would come in and calm him down. "It's only a phase he's going through dear."

"Brylcream, a little dab'll do ya." My little brother would whistle the jingle while I was doing my hair. It usually ended in a punch-up.

Spruso was good, but then I got onto this stuff called "Fixolene". You were set rock hard for a week.

My father hated my crewcut. He said it looked as if I got my hair mown every month.

The 1960s was the era of the beehive, a monstrous feminine creation in which hair was teased to the greatest possible height, smoothed over and then fixed with hair lacquer.

It had to be sprayed so it was solid, otherwise the top bits would fall off and you'd just be left with a mountain of teased hair.

We spent our time at school picking out split ends. It was a wonder we had any hair. We teased it mercilessly and nobody had ever heard of conditioner.

All the girls used Lustrecream shampoo to "look like a Hollywood star".

Sensible Undies

For girls, the beehive hairdo was the final touch in a wardrobe descended from the corsetry of the nineteenth century. Pantyhose, invented by a bright and free soul in the late 1960s, liberated girls from the bondage of suspender belts and step-ins.

The step-in was definitely a misnomer. You had to drag this thing up over your hips. To be effective, it had a circumference about 2 inches less than yours. It was made of the strongest elastic known to man.

Some of them actually had legs on them. I was fat and my legs used to bulge out where the step-in ended.

"Coca-Cola" and "Coke" are registered trade marks which identify the same product of The Coca-Cola Company.

The trouble with suspender belts was that they moved round your waist and your stockings would follow. You'd end up skew-whiff.

The worst thing was losing one of the suspender clips. The whole system would collapse. The step-in rode up and the stocking went down.

Women's underwear really was an aid to chastity. Apart from the fact you couldn't get them off, you wouldn't want anyone to know you had them on. But you were scared if you didn't wear them, you'd look fat.

When pantyhose came in, they were so hard to get that if one leg laddered, you'd chop off the defective leg and team them up with another pair.

I never got a bra that actually fitted. You were always told you needed support, or padding, or lifting or underwiring. The whole process was very demoralising.

There were a lot of dresses that needed strapless bras. They were amazing constructions that went down to the waist with bits of wire working loose and stabbing you. It was worse than having braces on your teeth.

1960s underwear was the art of looking totally alluring and being completely impregnable.

Dancing Class

The picture show, the milkbar and fellowship were all places for rendezvous with the opposite sex. But in spite of the advent of the rock and roll era, learning to dance properly was seen as a very necessary social grace. Once the Pride of Erin, the Military Two Step, the Foxtrot, the Tango, the Modern Waltz and the Cha Cha had been mastered, the teenager was supposedly ready for polite society.

Many a ship has been lost at sea,
For want of tar and rubber.
Many a girl has lost her boy,
From flirting with another.

I only agreed to go to dancing class because I knew boys would be there. The boys only went because girls were there. Unfortunately, everyone was too shy to speak.

The point of dance classes was so you could go to the dance class social night. Nobody really wanted to actually dance those dances.

All the girls wore gloves and the boys wore suits. We were allowed to wear very pale pink lipstick and matching nailpolish.

Once I'd been to dance classes and met all the right girls, my parents let me out at night. I went to rock concerts.

You Know You're Not Alone

Parental vigilance was not relaxed even when sufficient social graces had been acquired and the offspring could be trusted 'going out'. Surveillance continued.

Lee Gordon brought all these wild acts like Eddie Cochran and Little Richard out to Australia. That was when we began to escape Australian suburbia.

We were well brought up, well mannered little school girls. We went to the Beatles' concerts to scream.

My mother was a terror. She waited for the car to draw up and then sent my father out to water the lawn. She thought if he was out there, we wouldn't be necking in the car. It didn't occur to her that it might seem a little strange that someone would be watering the lawn at midnight.

"Parking places" were hard to find. The police felt quite free to come along and shine a light on you. If you looked young, they'd send you home and threaten to tell your parents.

A boy came to pick me up wearing sandshoes. We were only going somewhere informal, but my father told him to come back "properly dressed". I felt really humiliated.

We'd be standing on the porch and I'd wait for him to kiss me. Then the porch light would go on and I'd hear the upstairs window open. They wondered why I left home.

LOVE CAKE

2 oz of teasing
3 oz of squeezing
4 oz of kissing
Bake well in a young man's arms
  and serve him in the dark.
Use double ingredients if
  necessary.

CHAPTER NINETEEN

Pass the Parcel

Jingle bells, jingle bells,
jingle all the way.
Father Christmas lost his whiskers,
Smoking Craven A.

Christmas Traditions

'Temperatures reached the century today.' The news broadcasts around Christmas were invariably dominated by the climbing thermometer, the chance of a southerly, cricket and tennis scores. Cicadas drummed relentlessly, although Christmas beetles often left their appearance until the New Year. Christmas bush was cut and distributed round the neighbourhood. Bitumen roads bubbled in the sun. But nobody ever thought of having a beach holiday until after Boxing Day. The time prior to Christmas was spent sweating it out, waiting for the great event of the year.

For mothers, this meant concocting plum puddings from suet and glace cherries, struggling with calico pudding cloths and buying the chook. For children, it was a time of pants-wetting agitation. They watched as parcels were delivered to the house, only to be shoved onto the tops of wardrobes or secreted under beds. It was also a time of ritual — tree buying, tree decorating, putting out the cards, the school Christmas concert and buying Mum's and Dad's presents.

Mum was pretty competitive about the Christmas cards. The best ones went on the mantelpiece and on top of the piano. Our Venetian blinds nearly collapsed under the strain of the rest. I don't know what you did if you didn't have Venetian blinds.

The postman came twice a day. If an unexpected card arrived, Mum would send us along to post one off. She'd get furious

The obligatory visit to Santa.

with people who sent them just before Christmas. "Bloody Maud!", then there'd be a great scramble to get bloody Maud's card off in time.

The last Christmas delivery, the postie always came in for a drink. Mum gave him ten bob in an envelope and a cold beer. Everyone did it. God knows what state he was in by the end of the day.

The garbos and the dunny men got ten bob or a couple of bottles of beer. It wasn't safe to ignore them. You got garbage or worse spilt all over the drive.

Stage Fright

The school Christmas concert marked the end of the school year and the beginning of freedom. It was a time when emotions ran high.

I wanted to be Mary or an angel. I was too tall, so I always had to be a shepherd. But at least I was better off than my friend. The teacher told her she made a lovely sheep because of her curly hair.

Every year the teachers made a stage out of fruit boxes. They covered it with white crepe paper to symbolise snow. One year, as the choir started singing "Good King Wenceslas looked out", the fruit boxes started giving way. We were real troupers. We just kept singing as we crashed down, one by one. In the end, there were about three people left on fruit boxes and a lot of torn snow.

I was the innkeeper. I had to say, "I am the innkeeper. I am sorry, but I can only give you my stable." I rehearsed for a month, but on the night, my mind went blank. There was a dreadful pause and then everyone started hissing it at me from the side. I still couldn't get it. Finally Mary saved the night with a gracious "Thank you."

The Tree

Genuine plastic Christmas trees were a rarity. Real pine trees had to be bought from the fruit shop or from a roadside stall just before Christmas. Tree decoration had its dangers. The best decorations were made of fine, silvered glass, liable to disintegrate into sharp fragments in children's hands.

The little kids were only allowed to put the tinsel up. If you were older, you could stick on the gold stars, even though

Christmas concert — stage fright or rising stars?

they'd never stick properly. The best behaved person put the angel on top of the tree.

Every year we were at Mum to buy new tinsel. Last year's would be flat and stringy, grey and all knotted up. Mum always wanted to save money by having us make those silly paper loops you had on the tree at school.

You'd put the tree in a bucket with wet sand and lots of newspapers under it. If you bought it too early, it'd be going brown and dropping needles by Christmas. The worst thing was buying one that looked good in the shop and then finding it wouldn't stand up straight.

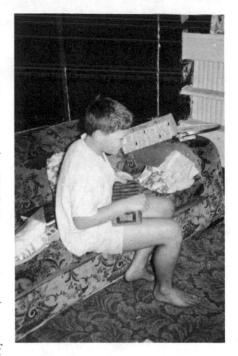

Unwrapping the presents was always the best part.

The Joy is in the Giving

Presents, rather than peace on earth and goodwill to all, were the point of Christmas for children. As the pile of presents grew under the tree, speculation ran rife as to what they contained. Apart from the 'big' present, from Mum and Dad, aunties, uncles and grandparents also made other worthwhile contributions.

You started off with a postal note for two and six from the aunts. As you got older, you moved up to five bob, then seven and six. After you were twelve, it settled, at ten bob. You might get a quid when you were fifteen or sixteen, then you just got socks or talcum powder like the rest of the family.

A postal note inside a Christmas card was the accepted gift from the aunties and uncles. We had one uncle who was a bit of a tearaway. He shoved the ten bob in the envelope. Everyone thought it was terribly risky. And just like him.

My grandmother gave me a marzipan fried egg, with a marzipan piece of bacon and a marzipan knife and fork, every single Christmas. It was great when I was three, but it was wearing thin by the time I was fifteen.

One of my aunts used to send ribbons, or lacy gloves or embroidered socks. They were only little things but they were the sort of things my mother never bought.

GIFTS FOR MOTHER

Small china poodle
Brooches that unfolded with views
of London Bridge
Brooches made of fake fruit
Six handkerchiefs embroidered
with 'flowers of Switzerland'
Embroidered handkerchief sachet
Foot powder
Matching bathcubes, soap and
talcum powder
Hand lotion
China ballerina
China Scotch terrier
1957 pocket diary
Comb in a case
China peasant girl
Weather vane with wet weather
man and the sunshine girl
Egg timer
Cup and saucer
Apron with 'Mother'
Potholder with 'Mother'
Tea towels
Souvenir teaspoon
Recipe book
Recipe folder

GIFTS FOR FATHER

Hankies
Tie
Socks
Shaving soap
Ashtray

Knock knock.
Who's there?
Mary.
Mary who?
Merry Christmas.

My mother must have swapped notes on what I needed for Christmas with my aunt. I used to get two pairs of socks and in return we'd send my cousin two pairs of socks.

My grandmother used to send me a handknitted jumper two sizes too small for me and a *London Illustrated* magazine. Mum said it would be cheeky to tell her about the jumper.

One of my aunts sent Mum bathcubes. Mum was furious. "How does she think I've got time to take a bath with six children?" But she kept them.

I always gave Dad hankies and a tie. I felt guilty because he never got much.

You'd go down the street after you opened your presents and see what everyone else got. I remember one really Christian family gave their kids Bibles. That was it. They had to be really happy about it too.

One girl got a new school uniform. There was nothing you could say.

Writing thank you notes was worst. How could you sound enthusiastic about six hankies?

The Christmas Feast

The Australian Christmas dinner has only become climatically civilised in recent years. In the post-war period, traditional Christmas fare was a hot roast, with all the trimmings followed by plum pudding and brandy sauce. It was most commonly served in the ninety degree heat in the middle of the day. Until the advent of the frozen chook, 'the bird' was the centrepiece of the main course.

The chook was always a big worry — whether it was going to be stringy or greasy. Mum and the aunties used to fuss endlessly, taking it in and out of the oven, basting it, checking its juices.

Mum would spend all morning in front of the stove and sit down, red-faced and exhausted. "I don't know why we bother with this," she'd say, But she'd insist on doing it every year.

We used to sit at a really long table and there'd be bottles of Victoria Bitter at intervals all along it, being passed back and forth. At the end of the meal, we kids were allowed to have a shandy on the grounds it'd send us off to sleep.

All the kids hated pudding, but we were all after the money. The adults all liked the pudding, but hated the money, because it chipped their false teeth.

One year, my little sister got all the money except one threepence. We nearly had a riot.

On Christmas night, we sat out on the verandah and picked at the chook bones. If it was hot, we kids went under the hose.

Happy Birthday to you,
You live in a zoo.
You look like a monkey
And smell like one too.

Birthday Parties

Birthdays were occasions for more concentrated and individual hysteria. Yet birthdays, like Christmas, were highly standardised, with little room for variation from the set pattern. The highlights were the presents and the party.

I always insisted on writing the invitations myself, absolutely determined to do them perfectly. I loved doing R.S.V.P. with a real flourish, but one would always smudge. I'd look at them before I gave them out and they'd all look really amateurish.

Giving out the invitations was the worst. Your mother would say you could only invite six people. There were always the kids who weren't invited to anybody's party. They'd be there when you were giving out the invitations. It made you feel bad.

Giving out the invitations for my tenth birthday, I couldn't get over the fact that I was ten. Double figures at last!

I loved getting dressed for parties. Even if it was after school, you went home and got into your best dress and wore your

If you wanted to eat you had to wear the hat.

Oranges and lemons,
Say the bells of St Clemens.
So when will you pay me?
Say the bells of old Bailey.
Today or tomorrow?
So chop off your head.

patent-leather shoes. If it was on a Saturday afternoon, Mum would do my hair in sausage curls. I always came home looking a wreck.

Birthday Food

Food was almost as standardised for birthday parties as it was for Christmas dinner. Mynor Fruit Cup cordial, GI Lime cordial or lemonade were standard drinks. Cocktail frankfurts and sausage rolls with large quantities of tomato sauce took care of most of the clean party dresses. Fairy bread, chocolate crackles, butterfly cakes, sponges and the birthday cake followed. Traditionally, the birthday cake was not eaten on the premises but taken home, wrapped in a serviette, into which it fused. Each guest was also given a small bag of lollies wrapped in cellophane. At a good party, you also got a balloon.

My mother once put out a plate of scones at my party. I felt really ashamed of her.

One year the boys started a tomato sauce fight. Mum never got the stain off the wall.

You could tell it was going to be a good party if they put lots of hundreds and thousands on the fairy bread.

One mother put SOS cough lollies in the lolly packets. We all thought that was pretty low.

I asked for another drink of cordial. The mother in charge pointed out I already had some. I tipped it onto the floor and said, "I haven't now." I got sent home. I don't know what got into me.

The first party I went to I got a balloon to take home. It was the first balloon I'd ever had. When it burst, I was devastated. I wanted to go back for another one. Mum said it would be forward.

Party Games

Food was usually preceded by games, with prizes for the winner. Blindman's buff, musical chairs, pin the tail on the donkey, drop the hanky, pass the parcel and oranges and lemons were played at almost every party. Parents attempted to keep these games orderly, usually without success.

My tenth birthday was a riot because one kid kept winning all the prizes. Everybody else revolted.

I won a whole bag of Fantales with blindman's buff. I felt truly wealthy.

The mother would come in with ten items on a tray. You got to look at them for about fifteen seconds. Then you had to write them down. The first one who got them all won.

There was a blindfold game called "Meet Lord Nelson". You'd be blindfolded and they'd tell you Lord Nelson had lost an arm at the Battle of Trafalgar and you were to shake hands with him. You'd end up shaking hands with a bent coathanger. Then you'd feel his wooden leg, which would be a curtain rod. By the time you got to his eye and were feeling a squashed grape, everybody would be killing themselves laughing and you'd be quite spooked.

I was good at musical chairs, but too enthusiastic. One day I missed the chair and crashed down so hard I cried. They felt sorry for me, so they gave me a prize anyway.

With "Pass the parcel", you could sometimes tell the parents were trying to help one of the kids win because they felt sorry for him . The rest always resented that.

Towards the end, the parties got wilder. There was always a game of kiss chasings. It was awful if you weren't caught.

The boys tied me to the towel rack in the bathroom with my sash. It was my best dress so I couldn't escape.

My parties were a disaster. I always ended up getting spanked and sent to my room. I was about ten before I realised birthdays weren't fun.

PARTY GAMES

Drop the hanky
Blindman's buff
Piggy in the middle
Oranges and lemons
Musical chairs
Pin the tail on the donkey
Pass the parcel
Bob the apple
Kiss chasings
Spin the bottle

CHAPTER TWENTY

Getting Wet

One day I went to the sea sea sea
To see what I could see see see.
But all that I could see see see
Was the bottom of the ocean
Sea sea sea.

Summer Holidays

To the baby boomers, as to children now, summer meant summer holidays. Summer holidays meant soaring temperatures and getting wet. Getting wet was important, whether it was under the hose, in the creek, the dam, at a burst fire hydrant or at the Olympic pool. In the post-war era, private pools were a rarity. The ultimate, of course, was the beach. For many families, a beach holiday was an annual event. But for the rest of the time, children had to find other ways of getting wet.

We used to go down to the creek. Even though it was very shallow, we were forbidden to swim. Mum would say. "You haven't been swimming in that creek again have you?" We'd shake our heads, forgetting our hair and our clothes were still damp.

To get to the creek, you had to go through the bush and you'd always get ticks. In the creek itself, there were leeches. In winter, it ran really fast, but by summer, it was just a pool, sometimes a bit stagnant. Still, it was water.

We used to climb the waterfall. It was strictly forbidden. I had a fight with one boy and he fell down. I justified it on the grounds he had freckles.

To get anywhere in summer, you had to have tough feet. You had to be able to walk on melting tar, hot sand and bindi-eyes.

188

By the end of summer, your feet were just right. Then, you had to go back to school.

You got dirty swimming in the dam. It was always muddy round the edge and slimy on the bottom. You were never quite sure if there was a yabby or an eel down there somewhere.

If a pipe burst in the road, you'd have kids just swarming there. It was like a miracle, water coming out of the road like that.

Dad used to water his vegetables after he came home from work. You'd walk past him on a hot night and he'd flash the hose round and squirt you. We'd get the other hose and start squirting back. Sometimes, the next door kids would get into the act and there'd be torrents of water everywhere. Mum would be on the back verandah screaming about not getting the clothes line wet.

When there were water restrictions on, you could only use the sprinkler between 6 and 7 o'clock. The kids would be up and down the street, running under hoses. One old duck down the road would always yell that the water was for the plants, not for us.

We had fantastic water fights. Mum filled up buckets in the bathroom and we kids ran out and tipped them over Dad. The

Who knew what lurked in the depths — or the shallows?

rest of us would be going mad with the hoses out the back. It was Dad against the rest of the family. He always won.

The Olympic Baths

In the 1950s, the public baths of the pre-war period gave way to Olympic pools, a trend accelerated by the Olympic Games fever of 1956. Whereas the old, pre-war baths were always slightly dank, with dark tiles and matching water, the new Olympic pools were bright blue-green and heavily chlorinated. Part of the improved education of the post-war era involved the 'learn to swim campaign'. In school time hordes of small, shivering, blue children resisted the 'breathe and bubble' campaign. In the holidays, the pools were packed to capacity with the same children, doing it their way.

There were always a whole lot of little kids down the shallow end of the big pool. They couldn't swim and they were too small to touch the bottom, but they didn't want to be in the babies' pool. They'd be hanging off the sides all day, edging their way round.

The chlorine was incredible. You came out with green hair and red eyes.

On a cold day, you'd go into the big pool until you were blue and shaking. Then you'd go and lie in the little pool to warm up.

Swimming underwater was the big thing. Some of us could go right across the pool without coming up. One boy was reputed to be able to do the whole length.

The deep end was supposed to be 20 feet deep. We were obsessed with being able to touch the bottom. It really hurt your ears. There's probably a whole generation of deaf people who spent their summers touching the bottom at the deep end.

Sometimes there was actually a serious diver on the top board. The rest of us were yahoos taking dares.

There was a line of kids running up to the top tower and jumping off, one after the other. It was amazing someone wasn't permanently disabled or killed.

There'd always be one bloke standing on the top board, preening and flexing. He'd always have incredibly brief black speedos.

The first time I went up to the top tower, I looked over and thought I can't. It was about a mile to the bottom. Then I looked back at my mates behind me. It was like a suicide pact. I jumped.

You actually weren't allowed to jump off the top tower. You were supposed to be a serious diver. One fellow was banned for jumping and went up there anyway. The guard was furious and screamed at him. "You get down from there." He did. He jumped.

There were signs everywhere, "No running on the concourse" and "No bombing", "No diving this end". The guards would send you to sit on the benches for ten minutes. If they caught you again, you'd be escorted to the turnstiles.

There was a sign as you went in, "Safety of valuables not guaranteed". We had no idea what it meant.

It cost a shilling to get in and sixpence for a locker. A locker seemed a waste of sixpence worth of lollies.

The locker lady only let you have one locker per person. Once she made my sister unpack her stuff. She found two towels and threatened her with the law.

The locker lady was about as mean as the guards. She'd only give you the key to the locker once if you wanted to get anything out. After that, you had to pay for another locker.

The Beach

The beach, as now, was the ultimate getting wet experience. The basic ingredients of sea, sun and sand

Of all the fishes in the sea,
I'd rather be bream at Circular Quay
To see the ladies swimming.

remain the same. The accessories are different and some of the habits have changed.

We had striped canvas beachbags with a drawstring top. They took your towel, your cap and your bathers.

The year we got proper beach towels! I hated taking our striped bathroom towels. My beach towel had "Hawaii" written on it. So sophisticated.

Thongs were really expensive when they first came in. Only one of our mates could afford them. He'd run over the hot sand and chuck them back. Then the next kid would run over and chuck them back.

If you wanted something more businesslike than an inner tube, you got a thing called a float. It was like a small, heavy duty blow-up mattress. Like bikes, you went up a size every year or so, and like bikes they got punctures. They had lethal valves at one end and you had to watch out if you were dumped.

My dad taught me to body surf. It was cissy to have a float or a tube.

I had an inner tube for surfing. It had no directional pull at all. After it was dumped on the sand a few times it went flabby.

Little kids used to wear the little blow-up tubes round their waists. I remember seeing my little sister floating out to sea, quite happily.

My father took me out to the big breakers. I was terrified. He'd push me off and I'd ride right into the shore. I'd forget how terrified I was and beg him to take me out again.

Families at the Beach

On the beach, every family had its umbrella. An umbrella not only gave shade, but also denoted territory and sometimes status. A faded umbrella was last year's umbrella. A tattered umbrella dated even further back. When the southerly came up, such distinctions lost their importance as all the umbrellas somersaulted dangerously along the beach, families in pursuit.

The umbrella marked your territory.

My Mum hated the sand and we'd always set up our umbrella in the park behind the sand. Behind the park, were benches on the side of the footpath. The 100-year-old people sat there and knitted.

The beach was the only place where we had takeaway food. Mum wouldn't let us have hamburgers. She said you didn't know what they put in them. We had fish and chips and pineapple fritters.

We set up the umbrella and stayed all day. Mum brought a picnic lunch: corned beef and tomato sandwiches. After lunch we weren't allowed to go back in the water for an hour. There were lots of cautionary stories about people going in straight after lunch, getting cramps and dying.

The best thing was to dig a really big hole and get yourself buried with only your head sticking out. The only trouble was that it took ages to get the sand out of your costumes.

Water Babies

Surfing and swimming, were the real reasons for the visit to the beach. The skill of body-surfing was highly respected, but surfboards became increasingly popular. They were large, difficult to transport and very heavy.

The cool set had boards and girls.

I wasn't worried about how I'd manage my first surfboard in the water. But it was so heavy that I couldn't see myself carrying it across the sand with any semblance of dignity.

I made my first surfboard from instructions in a magazine. My mate and I carried it to the water. It promptly sank.

You'd sit up on the beach, the surfboard next to you, smoking a Viscount, your girl sitting on the surfboard wearing a pink and white bikini. You really felt you'd made it.

Please Save Me!

Life savers, the archetypal bronzed Aussies, added both safety and glamour to the beaches. With far more primitive equipment than today, they worked long and hard hours. Unnetted beaches meant that sharks were an additional hazard.

I always wanted to get rescued by a life saver. When I did, he said, "Be more careful next time girlie." I felt a real idiot.

They had a watch tower on the beach. One of the life savers would be up there all the time, just watching the surf.

A rescue was really impressive. They had to swim out. There weren't any power boats.

The shark alarm was the most terrifying sound. You'd feel okay if there were people behind you. If you were a long way out and you could see everyone already on shore, it felt like real big trouble.

Tanning Torture

Sunburn was part of the Australian summer experience. Everyone knew it was painful, but no-one knew about

Local heroes on parade.

skin cancer. That was something only beach inspectors and old people got.

At the beginning of summer, I'd have no freckles. By the time I went back to school, my face would be covered with freckles. I used to think that if summer was long enough they'd all join up and I'd have a fantastic tan.

The bit I liked about getting a tan was having your swimming costume indelibly imprinted on your body. There was something really satisfying about it.

You used to feel sorry for the kids whose mother made them wear t-shirts *under* their swimmers. It looked really awful.

My mother swore by coconut oil. I'm sure it made your skin blister.

There was only white zinc cream. I hated having to wear it. It made you seem like a newcomer.

The zinc was really sticky. You had a coating of zinc then a coating of sand.

The sunburn was okay. It was the cure that killed you. Mum always said a good hot shower took the sting out. It took the sting out and your breath away.

Calamine lotion was supposed to be soothing. It may have been, but it shrivelled your skin at the same time.

Peeling was somehow satisfying. You'd tell your friends you were peeling. You'd feel superior if they weren't.

Beach Fashions

If sunburn protection was primitive, so too were beach clothes. Only gradually did swimming costumes actually become clothes suitable for getting wet.

Little girls had the bubble swimmers. They weren't terribly good for swimming but you could fill them up with water and they'd balloon right out.

There was a style with puffed-up pants for girls and an elasticised top. It was like a sundress gone mad.

You always knew the English kids because they had the black woollen togs with the white belt. You could tell just by looking at them that they wouldn't be able to surf.

The first lycra costumes were incredibly shiny. Unfortunately, the shine wore off in big patches, after you'd worn them a few times.

I was horrified when I got my first grown-up costume. It had a built in bra and all sorts of support. It was like wearing a boa constrictor.

The cotton speedos were really trim when you first got them. But then they sagged and faded to a dull blue. If you wanted to show your figure, you had to wear your last season's ones.

Mum made us wear swimming caps. They were heavy rubber and they really hurt. When you took them off, they pulled half your hair out.

My mother was crazy about swimming caps. She had a purple one with matching rubber flowers.

Getting There

Australia's capital cities are on the sea and for many baby boomers, going to the beach was a regular event. For others, the major seaside experience was the annual beachside holiday. Others used Dad's annual leave to go and visit the grandparents or cousins in the country. Getting to the country or to a beachside resort, was, in itself, a major expedition. Trains were important, but cars were the most common form of transport.

Every holiday we'd drive from Adelaide to Melbourne to see grandma. We'd never get there without a major breakdown.

Dad would say he heard something in the engine. You'd have an instant mental picture of standing by the road, in the heat, for hours while he was under the car, trying to find the noise.

We didn't have a car for ages. We finally got a Morris Minor with yellow plastic windows at the back. They all cracked after a while.

The dicky seats in the boot were tremendously exciting. We kids took turns to sit in them. You felt as if you were going twice as fast.

Blow-outs were really exciting. We seemed to have quite a few of them. The car would career off the road. Mum would be screaming. Somehow, Dad would stop the car. "It's only a blow-out," he'd say.

Whenever my mother was pulled up by a policeman, she explained she didn't have a licence. They seemed to think that was a reasonable excuse.

Dad always carried a vulcanising kit. He said he wouldn't feel safe without it. We felt safer too, even though we had no idea what it was.

It became very popular to have a rubber strip hanging down the back to stop car sickness.

Dad got really cross because we kids made him stop the car whenever we felt sick. He told us the next one who failed to be sick would be left on the side of the road. We all recovered immediately.

Five kids in the back of a little Austin. It was really crowded, there were no seatbelts and we fought. Dad would stop occasionally and belt us all. Then another riot would gradually build up.

You carried water in a canvas bottle with a ceramic top. It was hung at the front of the car. I think it was all those stories about people dying in the desert.

Train Trips

The two-car family was a rarity. In the post-war period, having one car was still something of a luxury. Many people still took their holidays at resorts near the train routes.

There were six kids in our family. The eight of us could just squeeze into one of those dog boxes on the train. Sometimes, we even got our own water bottle.

All the way to Sydney there were notices telling you how many miles it was to Griffiths Teas. We never went there, but it kept us entertained.

Changing at Albury in the middle of the night was great. The train on the Victorian gauge was waiting on the other platform. It made you feel you were really going somewhere different.

The trains had wooden shutters with adjustable slats. Trouble was, they weren't really adjustable. You'd try them out and then have to have them closed for the whole journey.

The country trains had tapestry blinds. You'd pull them up, stick your head out the window and get all the smoke and grit from the engine.

Holiday Stopovers

Motels first appeared in Australia in the second half of the 1950s. Until then, boarding houses — some good, some indifferent, some terrible — provided family accommodation. The only alternative was the country pub.

We stayed at a seaside boarding house every year. There were bingo and Irish dancing nights and cards and euchre. The same people went every year, so you got to know everyone.

Country pub breakfasts meant eggs and sausages with baked beans and bits of pineapple and beetroot and mountains of toast. One morning I counted eighteen different things on a plate of eggs and bacon. Great if you were a shearer, but it was horrible if you were a kid.

We stayed at pubs on our way up to Queensland. Some of them had the loo right out the backyard — awful if you were on the second storey and had to go in the middle of the night.

The first motel we stayed in amazed us. There was a bathroom to yourself and carpet on the floor. The most

At the boarding house fun was compulsory.

amazing thing was we ordered breakfast and it came through the servery hatch.

Up, Up and Away

In the post-war era, plane travel only very gradually became accessible to families for holiday travel. Many post-war children grew up with only a dream of flying. A lucky few actually experienced it.

You had to walk out on the tarmac and up the stairs into the plane. The first time, I was so excited, I wanted to run. My parents actually held me back.

The cabins weren't properly pressurised and you got an earache. They always gave the kids lollies.

Even my mother was amazed that they could serve food on a plane. I remember we got a Sao biscuit and a piece of cheese with fancy deckled edges. A miracle of modern cuisine.

The sick bags were the really interesting thing. On our first trip my brother and I discussed how much they'd hold, whether they'd actually hold it and what the air hostess would do with it. Finally my mother said, "Stop it you boys" and was sick into the bag. All our questions were answered.

I spent hours looking up at planes and imagining what it would be like to fly. When I actually did fly, I wished I could see the kids on the ground looking up at me.

I was really disappointed with my first flight. I thought you'd be able to open the windows.

Going to Camp

On the 'she'll be right' end of technology was camping. Some of children's most miserable experiences were in camps organised especially for children.

CAMP SONG

Flee
— Flee
Flee-fly
— Flee-fly
Flee-fly-flo
— Flee-fly-flo
Vista
— Vista
Goomala, goomala, goomala vista
— Goomala, goomala, goomala
   vista
Oh no nono nota vista
— Oh no nono nota vista
Eenimeena decimeena oowala
   wallameeny
— Eenimeena decimeena oowala
   wallameeny
Eximeena zollameena oowalawa
— Eximeena zollameena oowalawa
Beep diddley otten dotten bip bap
   a bitten batten, shhhh!
— Beep diddley otten dotten bip
   bap a bitten batten, shhhh!

I went to something called the National Fitness. All I can remember is that everyone cried, every night.

Camp was supposed to be a wonderful adventure. There was a big muddy lake which was a breeding ground for mosquitoes. The camp commandant told us children in other countries didn't have opportunities like this. Lucky them!

Happy campers on their way.

I counted the days. When Mum came to pick me up, I burst into tears. "Didn't you like it?" she said, as if she was really surprised.

The food was awful, it rained all the time and we spent an awful lot of time washing up.

The third time I went to camp, the food was a real surprise. You could actually eat it.

Camping with the Family

It was more fun camping with the family. As more Australian families bought cars, camping and caravanning became the new, popular and cheap way of holidaying.

We had one of those caravans made out of plywood, painted yellow and white. It was incredibly small for a family of six, but we took it away for the entire Christmas holidays. We lived on Heinz tinned spaghetti and had a wonderful time.

We used to park our caravan in Nanna's backyard. It seemed like cheating. I wanted to be down at the camping ground at the beach, with the other vans.

We had an old FJ Holden and we'd put the tent and the sleeping bags on the roof. Dad used to stop every ten minutes or so because he was convinced the ropes were working loose.

We had a big tent made of canvas and very heavy. It always leaked when it rained. The worst thing was getting up, out of a wet sleeping-bag, with no fire and having to pack up the wet tent.

We loved storms when we were in the tent. It'd be springing leaks and we'd be moving the sleeping-bags, digging trenches and putting saucepans under the leaks. When it got really bad, we slept in the car.

One night a tinned pudding exploded in the tent when Mum was cooking it. For years after we'd pick bits off the wall. My little sister always ate them.

Billy tea was part of camping.

Tempus Fugit

Mary had a little watch,
She swallowed it one day.
The doctor gave her castor oil,
To pass the time away.

Le croissant — a crescent shaped pastry roll eaten by the French for breakfast.

The baby boomer received this information somewhere between the ages of twelve and fifteen under the mysterious banner of 'French culture'.

Now comfortably ensconced in their designer kitchens, middle-aged baby boomers have croissants for breakfast. Supermarkets sell the No Frills variety, suitable for reheating in the microwave.

Le croissant is only a small example of Australia's metamorphosis into a multicultural society. Baby boomers, perhaps because of their Queen-loving, God-fearing childhood, have helped to create a society that is less than British to its bootstraps. They have turned Australia's cultural perspective away from Britain and have started to look at what it means to be Australian in a world context.

Baby boomers had a secure childhood. Compared to that of previous generations, it was prosperous. It may have been the predictability and security of their childhood that made the baby boomers think there must be more to life. They began to look at society critically and demanded the end to the White Australia policy. They created an environmental movement. Baby boomers demanded more generous social security and launched the anti-war, anti-nuclear movement. They became herbalists and went to encounter groups. The women created the women's movement. Like any generation, the baby boomer period had its ultra-radicals and its ultra-conservatives. Like any generation, it was divided within itself. But there is no doubt that from the mid-1960s,

In those days it was ham sandwiches and hard boiled eggs!

when baby boomers began to reach maturity, Australian society began to change radically.

'Quick,' calls the dying baby boomer. 'I'm an ex-Catholic. Call me an ex-priest.' The religious fall-out that occurred from the late 1960s was a radical change in Australian society. The baby boomer who attended mass as a child or went to fellowship as a teenager is likely to be anything — a lapsed Presbyterian, a Buddhist, a born again Christian, or a Hare Krishna.

Despite their soul-searching and idealism, the baby boomers are a generation of passionate consumers. Eschewing old-fashioned methods like saving up or lay-by, the baby boomer generation has created a credit-based society to equip itself with every conceivable domestic gadget from V.C.R.s and C.D. players to microwave ovens. Increasingly middle class and middle aged, baby boomers have nevertheless escaped the Aussie cultural cringe. As film goers and film makers, they have helped the renaissance of the Australian film industry. In the tradition of their childhood, they have continued to read voraciously. The difference is that our homegrown literature has finally lost its swaggies and billabongs. With their widened horizons and their plastic money, baby boomers have travelled extensively at home and abroad.

Their parents pursued the dream of the three bedroom brick veneer home almost to the exclusion of all else. It's on the baby boomers' agenda too, but now, it has a family room, en-suite bathrooms, a landscaped garden and an in-ground pool. And, of course, security locks.

The family home may be secure, but the actual family life of the baby boomer has become rather frayed round the edges. The pattern of family life has changed dramatically. Baby boomers did create their own miniature baby boom in the first half of the 1970s (all natural births please). But in general, they have opted for smaller families than those they grew up in — 2.1 children instead of 3.2. On the other hand, baby boomers have had husbands, wives and de factos in far greater numbers. Never have marriage and remarriage been so popular.

The baby boomers are giving their own children a very different childhood from the one they experienced. Some things, however, have been handed down. Baby boomers have passed on the music of their adolescence — the rock and roll of the sixties has proved remarkably persistent. They have also enshrined blue jeans as a standard item of dress. But the baby boomers' children face a different world. They are growing up in the computer age, with a confusing array of educational choices at the end of which there is no guarantee of employment.

Encapsulating a generation isn't easy, especially when it's still alive and kicking. Baby boomers came from a particular childhood in a particular era. They have radically changed the society in which they grew up. Yet, they have also retained some traditions. Supermarket shelves might be laden with freeze dried chow mein and Italian cooking sauce. Children are no longer dosed with castor oil and given junket for pudding. But, it's rumoured there are still a lot of baby boomers who insist on Vegemite on their croissants!

By hook or by crook,
I'll be the last in this book.

By Jack or by Jill,
I don't think you will.

Acknowledgments

This book was never researched in the formal sense. I make no apologies for this. Formal research proved to be unnecessary. Mention key words such as 'school milk', 'Meccano' or 'Vicks VapoRub' to a baby boomer and you can't stop them talking. My friends and acquaintances proved to be more than generous with their memories.

I did hold a series of dinner parties, dubbed the Australian childhood dinners. These events usually ended very late with participants convulsed with laughter about fluorescent socks, sex education or billycart races. Sometimes, we had licorice allsorts and musk sticks for dessert.

I would like to thank the following people for their participation in and contributions to this book:

Lindsay Anderson, Carl Askew, Sue Bradley, Brian Bowden, Julia Cain, John Carmody, Jonathan Chester, Jenny Colwill, Colleen Cooke, Mary Draper, Bruce Hancock, Julia Irwin, Dean Letcher, Robyn Lewis, Elizabeth Maher, Alison McIntyre, John McIntyre, Kirsty Melville, Cathy Munro, Stephen O'Bryan, Bill Pepper, Judy Russell, Leonie Thompson, Lance Tomlinson, Dave Townsend, Jill Townsend, Rosanna Townsend, Simon Townsend, Jim Yeo, Pat Yeo. Thanks to Jane, Tom and Chris Bertinshaw for supplying photographs and Meccano, and to Ken Stewart for the matchbox cars and building the Meccano vehicle. Special thanks to my resident baby boomer, Steve Townsend, not only for his excellent and lurid memory, but also for his help and encouragement throughout the project.

Photographs and Pictures

I gratefully acknowledge the permission of the following for use of photographs and pictorial material:

Impey family (pp. 6, 12, 15, 44, 51, 86, 90, 123, 128); Bertinshaw family (pp. 8, 107, 185); Commonwealth Bank for the advertisement from *The Australian Women's Weekly*, 15 July 1950 (p. 9);

Hills Industries Limited (p. 13); Carl Askew (pp. 19, 36, 95, 183, 200); Education Department of NSW (pp. 19, 26, 32, 60, 76, 182); Stephen Townsend (pp. 20, 46, 158, 166); Judy Russell (pp. 21, 30, 74); Parker Pen (Australia) Pty Limited for the advertisement from *The Australian Women's Weekly*, 24 June 1950 (p. 24); Jonathan Chester (p. 31); Gould League of Bird Lovers (p. 32); Australian Red Cross (pp. 34, 129, 202); Colleen Cooke (p. 35); Reckitt & Colman Australia Ltd, Foods division, for the Keen's Curry advertisement from *The Australian Women's Weekly*, 19 August 1959 (p. 37); *Woman's Day* magazine for the illustration from *Woman's Day with Woman*, 7 November 1960 (p. 40); Traders Pty Limited for the Aeroplane Jelly packet (p. 42); David Jones Pty Ltd (pp. 49, 50, 53, 92, 94, 109, 162); Reckitt & Colman Australia Ltd, Pharmaceutical division, for the Dettol advertisement from *Woman's Day*, 12 November 1962 (p. 55); The Royal Alexandria Hospital for Children (pp. 62, 106); Mentholatum Pty Ltd for the Laxettes advertisement from *Woman's Day*, 3 September 1962 (p. 63); BML Pharmaceuticals Pty Ltd for the Ford Pills advertisement from *The Australian Women's Weekly*, 15 July 1950 (p. 66); The Wrigley Company Pty Limited for the Wrigley's Spearmint Chewing Gum advertisement from *Woman's Day with Woman*, 1 June 1959 (p. 68); *The Sydney Morning Herald* (pp. 69, 87); Rosanna Townsend (pp. 77, 172, 181); Julia Cain (p. 78); W.D. & H.O. Wills (Australia) Limited for the cigarette packets (p. 83); Ariana Klepac (pp. 91, 154, 203); *Herald and Weekly Times* (pp. 98, 102, 112, 113, 125); McIntyre family (pp. 100, 121, 193); Icarus Klepac (p. 101); Townsend family (p. 118); Hans van Pinxteren (p. 132); Brisbane City Art Hall and Museum (p. 132); National Film and Sound Archive and Joan Sheil (p. 135); Rank Organisation for the still from the film *Bush Christmas* (p. 137); General Television Corporation Pty Ltd for the still from the film *Long John Silver* (p. 138); Australian Broadcasting Commission (pp. 141, 144, 153); Glenn A. Baker and 2GB Pty Ltd (p. 146); National Library of Australia (pp. 147, 189, 194, 195, 205); Channel 10, Sydney, for the still from the program *Daniel Boone* (p. 150); Hodder & Stoughton, United Kingdom, for the illustration by Eileen Soper from the 1967 edition of *Five Go Off in a Caravan* by Enid Blyton (p. 157); Angus & Robertson Publishers for the Frank P. Mahony illustration from the 1920 edition of *Dot and the Kangaroo* by Ethel C. Pedley (p. 159); Family Life Movement for extracts and illustration from *The Guide to Virile Manhood* and *A Guide to Womanhood* (pp. 167, 168); Simon Townsend (pp. 170, 172); John Carmody (p. 171); Coca Cola Australia Pty Ltd (p. 176).